CYBERATTACK

First published in 2014 by Carlton Books
Carlton Publishing Group
20 Mortimer Street
London W1T 3JW
Text copyright © Paul Day 2014
Design copyright © Carlton Books 2014

A catalogue record for this book is available from the British Library

ISBN-13: 978-1-78097-454-5

Printed and bound by CPI Group (UK) Ltd, Croydon, CR0 4YY

CYBERATTACK

The truth about
digital crime, cyber warfare
and government snooping

PAUL DAY

CARLTON
BOOKS

Dedications

I'd like to thank my wife for her constant patience and tolerance of a man who can be manic and obsessional when researching and writing.

I'd like to thank my parents, who encouraged me to think and question from an early age, despite the problems it caused them.

I'd like to thank my mentors, Professors Martin Atkinson and Noel Sharkey, who tried to refine my raw talent into something useful.

I'd like to thank all the people at Carlton Books who have helped me over the years: Martin Corteel, who gave me my first chance to write; Roland Hall, who helped me to write more; Matt Lowing, who has shown the patience of a saint while encouraging me to write this book; and James Pople for the book's striking design. Special thanks to Malcolm Croft, whose editing and input was invaluable.

Finally, I'd like to thank a good and true friend, Kris Ward of Cybatek systems. He knew me better than I knew myself when he encouraged me to buy "a box with buttons on" back in 1983. That was the moment that changed my life forever. Without Kris Ward, this book would never have been written.

Paul Day
October 2013

About the Author

Paul Day is a veteran IT specialist and "old school" hacker who has worked with computers for over 30 years and has been described by the BBC as an "author and chronicler of the hacking scene". Trained in Cognitive Psychology, Psycholinguistics and Artificial Intelligence, he soon spotted the potential of the internet and began learning TCP/IP before the World Wide Web had been developed. He later worked as part of the team that developed the prototype Oyster Card and then became an IT specialist for what *The Times* has called "The World's Most Famous Secret Society." A long time attendee of the *London 2600* group, he co-founded the hacker electronic magazine P/H-UK with the notorious hacker Zap before quitting the hacking scene. He is the author of the bestselling *Hackers' Handbook* and *Hackers' Tales*.

CONTENTS

SECTION FOUR: Cyber Protection

Discussing the cyber world inevitably means using technological or specialist terms that may be unfamiliar to the general reader. Such terms appear in the Glossary and are set **bold** when first used in the text

INTRODUCTION

CYBER THREAT

We are all living in an age of perpetual cyber threat. We no longer trust our computers – and everybody is at risk.

Twenty years ago the level of cyberthreat was minimal. The threat landscape was comprised of hobbyist **hackers** who ruled the net and waived the rules. Now, everything has changed. The threat is no longer a few tech-geek, old-school hackers who wanted to explore and do nothing more. Now the **internet** itself is the threat. Cyberthreat is everywhere. The threat is in your pocket. The threat is in your home. The threat is inside the servers you use every day to communicate online. The threat is inside the telephone system. The threat is inside the **Supervisory Control and Data Acquisition (SCADA)** systems that control our public utilities. The threat is inside the systems that control our money.

Cyberthreat is everywhere and nowhere – because the threat is inside the system itself and there is nothing we can do to stop it. **Cyberspace** itself is a threat and the internet has become the engine of a modern cyberwar.

It is not just in your computer, not just in your pocket. It is also possibly in your toilet and fridge – and even your pacemaker, if you have one. There are currently an estimated 8.7 billion connected devices in the world – and each one is a threat to the owner. It has been estimated that this will grow to 15 billion devices by 2015, and 40 billion by 2020.

Everybody who connects to the internet is at risk. Estimating the number of webpages on the internet is difficult because there are no reliable statistics. According to the daily statistics provided by WorldWideWebSize.com, there were at least 1.31 billion pages in October 2013. Kevin Kelly, one of the founders of *Wired* magazine, has written that there were at least a trillion web pages on the internet in 2011. Because nobody knows the exact size of the World Wide Web, an organisation founded by Tim Berners-Lee, who invented the HTML and HTTP protocols that underpin the World Wide Web, started a project in 2011 called the "World Wide Web Index" to determine the number of webpages in existence. What we do know is that the 2012 Netcraft survey discovered that there were 644 million active websites on the internet. Each one of those websites and each one of those webpages are a potential threat to a web browser.

Everybody who uses cyberspace is at risk and it doesn't matter which type of computer or operating system you use. It doesn't matter whether you use a desktop, a laptop, a smartphone, a tablet or an online gaming console. The risk is *inside* the system. The risk is the result of a culture of permanent "always-on" inter-connectivity. The risk is part of the huge growth of the internet in the last twenty years. Risk is everywhere in the digital world.

Looking back on it now, it seems astonishing that the internet – the technological playground of scientists, the military and early hackers – would have been so popular. In the early eighties, computers were seen as a passing fashion, a pastime for hobbyists and electronics aficionados. By the early nineties, computers were everywhere, but the internet was viewed as nothing more than a fad, a techno-geek-boy fantasy that had appeal for very few people.

Thomas J Watson, the chairman of IBM in 1943, has been famously identified though never verified, as the man who said, "I think there is a world market for maybe five computers". Which is on a par with the comment of Dick Rowe, who passed up the chance to sign *The Beatles* saying "We don't like their sound, and guitar music is on the way out".

Large corporations are often slow to see the income potential of modern technological changes. But, if there is one thing to be said about futuristic predictions, they are almost all wrong. After all, there are no flying cars in my garage and I have never used a personal jet-pack to commute to work.

These days we take the internet for granted. Businesses and corporations soon spotted the potential of the internet for advertising and marketing. Early websites were often rough and ready, but the advertising and marketing gurus soon did their homework and smoothed off the rough edges. As cyberspace grew rapidly, it was soon discovered that for advertising and marketing the internet was the **fifth domain** – fifth after the well established techniques of billboards, press, radio and television. Today we live in a world of permanent connectivity and the risk of cyber attack is real. The price we pay for the use of internet giants such as Facebook, Twitter, and Google is that we must learn to live with the following cyber threats on a daily basis.

Cybercrime

The first major cyber threat is **cybercrime**. In times of economic crisis cybercrime is a growth industry. Ever since the birth of the internet and the invention of the World Wide Web, there has been cybercrime. The use of computers and digital communications for hacking, piracy, pornography and copyright theft have existed in cyberspace from the beginning. What is extraordinary is the huge parallel growth in financial cybercrime – the genesis of a "digital mafia" that seeks only monetary gain. The huge expansion of the World Wide Web has allowed large numbers of **cyber-criminals** to make small fortunes from the cybercrime industry. Cybercrime pays if you don't get caught – and the chances of getting caught are still very small – despite the best efforts of global anti-cybercrime agencies and the digital cybercops.

The growth in cybercrime is paralleled by the growth of the web itself. As newbie users begin to use the internet, they are seen as nothing more than "fresh meat" by cyber-criminals and **black hat hackers**. The annual growth of potential victims of cybercrime – who have no idea how to protect themselves in the savage online world called cyberspace – represents nothing more than easy-pickings for experienced cyber-criminals. Someone, possibly P T Barnum once said, "There's a sucker born every minute". In cyberspace there are hundreds of new victims born every second.

A reliable source of statistics on the growth of cybercrime can be found by reading the annual IC3 reports. The Internet Crime Complaint Centre (IC3), was founded in 2000 as a joint effort between the National White Collar Crime Center (NW3C)/Bureau of Justice Assistance (BJA) and the Federal Bureau of Investigation (FBI). The figures speak for themselves: since 2001 the overall cost of cybercrime in the US has risen from

$17.1 million to an estimated $485.3 million[1] – although some security experts allege the costs are higher due to the large number of unreported cybercrimes by online banking institutions. The current estimates for the year 2013 place the possible US losses as high as $500 million. Globally the figures are much higher: although nobody knows the true figures – it could reach as high as $2 billion by 2013 and the trend is upwards. Some industry estimates place the costs as high as $1 trillion.

But these figures are the direct losses to industry and individuals – it does not include the hidden costs of extra law enforcement, upgraded security programs and the direct cost to internet users for anti-virus, anti-malware, firewall and other security related software. It turns out that the true cost of cybercrime is much higher than the estimates – a finding which impacts every internet user of the planet and has profound effects on the growth of online trade, banking and services. The slower growth of online commerce – caused by the lack of consumer confidence – could mean that cybercrime is costing global commerce around $4 billion per year in lost business.

Cybercrime has funded the rise of a New Dark Economy, where the installation of **remote access trojans (RATs)** facilitates the theft of banking information – allowing the theft of up to $3,000,000 in a single digital heist. The digital mafia is the cyber-equivalent of organised crime, with a boss and an organisation such as the Russian Business Network as allies. Normal cyber-criminals are more disorganized, using internet cybercrime forums as a **force multiplier** which connects buyer to seller, cash-out mule to credit card seller and more. Although the digital mafia grabs media headlines with large organised digital heists, the real threat is digital disorganized crime which steals little but often; they understand that the art of cybercrime is not getting caught. The cybercrime economy supports Black Software Laboratories – whose only aim is to write **malware**. In the "Darkside Silicon Valley" of evil software, there is only one question: Who will be the cybercrime equivalent of Microsoft?

1 The IC3 was originally called the Internet Fraud Complaint Center (IFCC) and was subsequently renamed the Internet Crime Complaint Center (IC3) in December 2003.

Cyberwar

The second major cyber-threat is cyberwar. Who is attacking our computers? Hacktivists, cyber-terrorists and cyber-warriors are a modern threat in cyberspace. The trend towards modern digital warfare by many countries is obvious. Modern power blocs, such as the USA, China, Russia and Israel, are actively researching, building and deploying cyber weapons. The new generation of cyber attacks, using weapons such as **Stuxnet**, can reach into the very heart of our society, denying us access to the utilities we take for granted. The state-of-the-art cyber attacks on utilities, transportation, communication and financial systems can be used to cripple the economy of a country and bring it to a standstill without a single shot being fired.

Do not believe that the cyberwar is virtual. Cyberwar can cause damage to society far beyond anything that we have ever seen before. If a real cyberwar breaks out – and cyber weapons are deployed – we will no longer have to worry about updating our Facebook or Twitter status. We will be more worried about withdrawing our cash from ATMs, buying food and the lack of electricity and water. The cyber arms race is underway and if your computer, smartphone or website gets destroyed, that is nothing more than "digital collateral damage". As long ago as 2006, it was estimated that 120 countries led by the USA, Russia and China were developing cyber weapons, but after the Stuxnet incident, that number must have grown. The truth is that nobody really knows, because preparations for cyberwar are mostly shrouded in secrecy, even in democracies such as the USA and UK. There is a thriving market for hackers who discover vulnerabilities in systems and then sell the information to the highest bidder. Nation states are preparing themselves for cyberwar and the risks of cyber attacks are increasing every year.

Once unleashed these cyber weapons will provide the blueprint for every terrorist organization on the planet. The programming source code for Stuxnet can be downloaded by anyone with an internet connection, then simply modified and re-used. Destructive cyber weapons that attack national infrastructure are going to become a terrorist's standard issue. Like the AK–47 or the car bomb, they are a powerful force multiplier that allows a terrorist group to inflict an asymmetrical amount of damage to an enemy. The use of cyber weapons allows anybody a degree of plausible deniability, preventing political blowback. The possibility of using cyber weapons makes them a good option for nation state actors in the new digital covert wars. If Russia launches a cyber attack on the USA national infrastructure using Chinese cyber weapons from computers hosted in China, who will the USA blame?

Cyber-paranoia

The third major cyber-threat is the evolution of the internet as a tool of **perpetual surveillance**, which could cause irreparable damage to or even destroy modern democracy and civilization. In the post 9/11 era, the American War on Terror and the generation-long war against Islamic terrorism have had a deep and lasting impact on the internet and global communications. Despite the Obama administration distancing itself from "War on Terror" rhetoric – noting that the phrase is neither useful nor correct – there has been no decrease on domestic spending on intelligence programs designed to routinely monitor citizens.

Instead, there have been new efforts to intercept virtually everything that occurs on the internet, with the major internet companies assisting the US government by allowing access to private data held on their servers. This new digital counter-insurgency, the struggle against the 'enemy within', is being fought in information-space. The weapons are powerful computers that collect, collate and store vast amounts of data. Citizens are monitored continually with CCTV cameras, and powerful computers using sophisticated AI-based algorithms can extract facial and number plate information within seconds.

These modern techniques of surveillance in the name of the War on Terror redefine cyber-threat. Now the threat is *you* – even if you are innocent you are presumed guilty. The growth of automated AI-based surveillance and **data-mining** techniques across the internet mean that computers number and profile everybody on the planet. Government-based internet surveillance programs – such as **PRISM** – do not make us safer. The evidence suggests that even if you have nothing to hide, you still have everything to fear. You are just a profile in a computer somewhere in a huge counter-terrorist database. Does that make you feel safer?

If we give up our rights to security and privacy – and it changes our civilization – have the terrorists won after all? Consider this: Financial transactions are data-mined for patterns that fit the profile of terrorists, drug dealers and money launderers. Anyone who fits the profile automatically becomes a suspect – but the profiling always isn't correct. The 2006 case of Walter Soehnge, a retired Texas schoolteacher, who sent in a cheque for $6,522 to pay off part of his credit card bill and subsequently received a visit from the Department of Homeland Security, shows that even if you have nothing to hide you always have something to fear. For this reason the growth of ubiquitous, systematic, automated surveillance technologies is one of the biggest threats that democracy faces.

Who programs these systems? Who has access to these systems? Is the data confidential? What if the computers make a mistake? How reliable are these automated systems designed to monitor our everyday movements and what are the chances of these data-mining systems determining that you are the *threat* – while ignoring actual terrorist plots?

Do these automated systems make us less or more secure? The vast automated systems that analyze data for security purposes not only places law-abiding

When everybody is perpetually watched by computers that decide if our patterns of behavior fit a terrorist profile, then everybody is a potential security threat.

citizens at risk of arrest, funds-seizure or worse, but for every 2,750 law-abiding citizens that are persecuted there could be 10 terrorist plots going on undetected. Do you feel safer now that you know that you are being watched all the time?

This is the new virtual fear of the modern age: Who controls the data that controls our lives?

As the War on Terror accelerates, the problems associated with a permanent surveillance culture in a digitally interconnected world are already being felt. When everybody is perpetually watched by computers that decide if our patterns of behavior fit a terrorist profile, *everybody* is a potential security threat. The underlying assumption behind all of these systems is that *nobody* is truly innocent, that everybody is a potential mole, a potential sleeper, a potential drug dealer, a potential terrorist or a potential money-launderer. Examining the recent developments in computerized surveillance techniques leads to a frightening conclusion:

when everybody is perpetually watched as a potential terrorist suspect, we *all* become "the enemy".

As we take for granted the perpetual surveillance and intrusions into our privacy that were previously only the realm of science-fiction we are living in an information dystopia that far outstrips anything that George Orwell imagined. Will the technological developments designed to save democracy end up destroying it?

Cyber Attack is about our collective modern paranoia about the online world. It is about how we take for granted the devices and computers we use in the information age, and so open ourselves up to a world of digital risk. When the tools we use on a daily basis become invisible in our modern world, we are all at risk.

The effect of modern, cyber-threat is to undermine the utility of computers, networks and the internet as a means of communication. Computer users already have to worry about security and use firewalls, anti-virus, anti-spyware, anti-adware and anti-rootkit software – but it is necessary to go further. To understand the impact of the internet-connected devices on our lives, we need to evaluate the risks and act accordingly.

The growth in modern cyber-threats can be reduced only when users learn to secure their computers from the very first moment they attach it to the internet. For this reason every internet user has a responsibility to ensure that their computer is secure as possible. Once users make a commitment to a local system security, it benefits not only them but every other internet user, by preventing **viruses**, **spam**, worms and **botnets** from spreading. Denying the low-hanging fruit of unsecured computers to cyber-criminals, cyber-terrorists and cyber-warriors is the first step towards a safer, more secure internet. By securing your own computer, you can become part of the solution and not be part of the problem. If you allow your computer to be infected with malware, it could damage everyone who connects to you – with horrifying consequences.

Although the current state of virtual fear is a real and present danger, it seems that the majority of users prefer to take no action, rather than evaluating the risks and formulating an appropriate response.

SECTION 1

CYBERCRIME

"Cybercrime is one of the greatest threats facing our country, and has enormous implications for our national security, economic prosperity, and public safety."

US Department of Justice, 2013

Cybercrime is a low risk and potentially highly profitable illegal business and cybercrime is now the number one cyber threat on the internet. This section describes the major types of cybercrime and explores the New Dark Economy that drives the activities of cyber criminals.

1

CYBERCRIME DEFINED

Cybercrime has replaced hacking as the number one threat on the internet. Telecommunications and computer crime are not new. Hackers and Phone Phreaks have been abusing the phone network and internet for many years now. What is new is the motivation behind the criminal activities. Early phreakers and hackers wanted to explore communications systems because of intellectual curiosity – cyber-criminals hack because they want to make money. Whatever the motivation, the tools and techniques used by hackers and cyber-criminals are very similar, but the cyber-criminals write **crimeware** whose only purpose is to make money.

What is Cybercrime?

Why "cybercrime"? Surely "computer crime" or "internet crime" would be a better choice of words? To understand why this is important we need to begin with a simple question:

What is cyberspace?

In 1984, William Gibson published *Neuromancer* – a novel that popularized the term "cyberspace" – and is still widely regarded by hackers as one of the most influential science fiction novels of all time. In this futuristic story cyberspace is a direct neural connection into a virtual reality, a consensual hallucination that could be shared by everyone on the planet. While ordinary people used cyberspace for work, future hackers called "cowboys" roam cyberspace stealing data and money for profit. In a real sense Gibson not only invented cyberspace but also the very idea of cybercrime itself. *Neuromancer* had a huge impact on the hacking scene and is possibly the most important vector for spreading the "hacker" meme alongside *Wargames* (1983). The ideas contained in *Neuromancer* have become common currency in the modern world and the use of the term "cyberspace" is possibly the most important.

Fellow cyber-punk science fiction author Bruce Sterling has applied the ideas of cyberspace to the modern world – and we can paraphrase them for the twenty-first century.

- Cyberspace is the "place between the places that we all use to communicate in the modern world".
- Cyberspace is the place where "digital communications appear to occur".
- Cyberspace is not inside modern digital devices. It is not inside your smartphone, laptop or desktop computer.
- Cyberspace is not inside another person's digital device, either in their pocket or on their desk.
- Cyberspace is not just the internet; the phone system, the largest machine on the planet, is also part of cyberspace.

Cyberspace is the place between the places: an undefined space that allows communication across multiple digital devices and across multiple digital pathways – to provide the illusion of instant communication. Cyberspace is both everywhere and nowhere at the same time, which makes it a slippery idea to grasp. We all know what cyberspace is – but it seems not to exist at all.

The author Michael Lind has suggested that "there is no such place as cyberspace," and that "it is a bad metaphor that has outlived its usefulness". He argues cogently that "using the imagery of a fictitious country makes it harder to have rational arguments about government regulation or commercial exploitation of modern and communications technologies". Lind might well be on the right track but mistaking "countries" for "concepts" and suggesting that the "physical" and the "real" are one and the same is missing the point. This does nothing to advance the debate about the meaning of the word cyberspace. Like it or not, that strange wonderland called cyberspace has arrived and is here to stay. If treating the internet as a mythical country makes us dumber, then ignoring the reality of the cyberspace metaphor makes us dumber still. Cyberspace may not exist in a conventional sense – and maybe the cyber-metaphor has out lived its usefulness – but cyber-criminals commit cybercrimes in cyberspace every day. These cybercrimes, committed in the nowhere land of cyberspace, have an impact on the real world because real money is stolen.

Luckily, governments are less concerned about whether cyberspace exists or not – they have to plan homeland defence and defend against cyber-terrorists and cyber-criminals. Lawyers and law enforcement need to plan legal strategies to identify, apprehend and prosecute cyber-criminals. Both groups need a definition of cyberspace that is fit for purpose.

This is the real difference: cyberspace is not a foreign country or a mythical land. Cyberspace is a human construct that is infinitely malleable by both operators and skilled hackers.

The National Security/Homeland Security Presidential Directives NSPD-54 and HSPD-23 (2008) defined cyberspace as, "the interdependent network of information technology infrastructures, and includes the internet, telecommunications networks, computer systems and embedded processors and controllers in critical industries." In that same year a Deputy Secretary of Defense Memorandum defined cyberspace as a "global domain within the information environment consisting of the interdependent network of information technology infrastructures, including the Internet, telecommunications networks, computer systems, and embedded processors and controllers." Legal experts interested in cybercrime such as Susan W. Brenner point out that, "cyberspace is not a fixed, predetermined reality operating according to the principles which cannot be controlled or altered by man. The cyberworld is a constructed world, a fabrication. Because it is a construct, cyberspace is mutable; much of it can be modified and transformed".[2] This is the real difference: cyberspace is not a foreign

---

2 Susan W. Brenner, "Organized Cybercrime? How Cyberspace May Affect the Structure of Criminal Relations," *North Carolina Journal of Law & Technology* Vol. 4 No. 1

country or a mythical land. Cyberspace is a human construct that is infinitely malleable by both operators and skilled hackers.

This intangibility of cyberspace, the fact that it is both real and imaginary, leads to multiple problems when dealing with modern cybercrime. The major problem is that cybercrime is transnational in nature. A hacker in the USA will steal credit card credentials and then sell them on the black market to fellow cyber-criminals across the globe. Those cyber-criminals can then use "cash-out mules" to withdraw money from ATMs around the world in a single day – the cash-out mules typically earn around 20 per cent commission – and the money is then wired to the cyber-godfathers behind the scam using money transfer services. To crackdown on this type of digital disorganized crime, there needs to be transnational cooperation between the law enforcement agencies in possibly a dozen countries, some of which have few or no laws restricting hacking and cybercrime. Many countries such as Russia have refused to sign the 2001 Budapest Convention on cybercrime and those countries are now "safe havens" for modern digital cyberthieves providing services and malware to anyone in the world who can pay.

Botnet herders based in Spain build botnets such as the Mariposa and then hire them out to other cyber-criminals to send spam or mount **Distributed Denial of Service (DDoS)** attacks. The cyber-criminals hiring the services of the Botnet herder do not have to be in the same country – they can be based anywhere on the internet – and still use the botnet. Of course, an added complication is that the botnet itself (composed of hundreds or thousands of computers) is widely distributed across the globe in the form of compromised **zombie** computers. Tracking down and dismantling a botnet of this type requires massive cooperation – not just by law enforcement but also by security experts. In order to isolate and take down the botnet command and control server, the malware code needs to be analyzed. To track down the culprits behind the botnet server requires online digital detective work. Sometimes, even after all that work, there is insufficient evidence to prosecute the botnet herders and they go free. If they live in a country with few or no laws against cybercrime, they also go free. Cybercrime is a low risk and potentially highly profitable illegal business. Small wonder cybercrime is now the number one cyber threat on the internet.

Cyber-criminals have quickly learned how to steal in cyberspace – and the "triangle of cybercrime" relies on three things: (1) the generation of possibilities for cybercrime through data theft and malware introduction; (2) the operation and maintenance of cyber-criminals through a secondary supply chain; and (3) a seemingly endless supply of low level cyber-criminals and "cash-out mules" who are the foot soldiers in the cyber-mafia – and who get caught eventually. Successfully combating cybercrime requires law enforcement and security researchers needing to attack each corner of the triangle simultaneously – denying cyber-criminals malware, income and willing foot soldiers.

Another problem with the nature of cybercrime is defining what is actually stolen. Sometimes nothing is stolen because the original data is still available. Stealing data is not like stealing a television, which deprives the victim of the television. Stealing data takes a copy of the data, leaving the original intact. Sometimes the victim doesn't even know they have been stolen from until it's too late.

According to a study by the Annenberg School for Communication, the problem is increasing. In 2002, the amount of stored digital data in the world finally reached the same point as the amount of analog stored information. By 2007, stored digital information accounted for an astonishing 94 per cent of the world's known recorded information. According to global analysts IDC, in 2012 the total amount of digital information in the world was 2.7 zettabytes – that's 2.7 followed by 21 zeros. As *Forbes* journalist and information security specialist Andy Greenberg points out, "And all of that information is *liquid:* infinitely reproducible, frictionlessly mobile – fundamentally leakable."

When 94 per cent of the world's information is digital, it doesn't take much to tip the balance of civilization into a "New Dark Age". If cyber-criminals bring our society to a halt through ill-advised use of malware and RATs, nobody will be able to get any money from the ATMs and purchasing using a credit card will become impossible.

A 2010 study of the annual Cyber Security, by Deloitte, made the danger quite clear. "Data is more valuable than money. Once spent, money is gone. But data can be used and re-used to produce more money. The ability to reuse data to access on-line banking applications, authorize and activate credit cards, or access organization networks has enabled cyber-criminals to create an extensive archive of data for ongoing illicit activities". It should be noted that hacktivists like **Anonymous,** and their ilk, refuse this paradigm. For them, data is to be shared to the point of devaluation. When everybody knows your secrets, the secrets are worthless and the data can no longer be reused and it has no further value.

The difficulty of defining cybercrime accurately, except by an exhaustive list of possible cybercrime types, makes it difficult to accurately assess the scale of the problem. In 2001 the Budapest Convention on Cybercrime recognized the need for international co-operation of security companies and law enforcement – but listed only 11 major types of cybercrime.

The FBI currently track cybercrime types using 27 different categories of cybercrime – but there are more than 60 sub-categories. Different law enforcement agencies across the world have different cybercrime laws – and some countries have no laws at all. Once again the distributed transnational nature of cybercrime makes it harder to prevent than ordinary crime.

Every year, digital scam artists think up new ways to steal money by infecting our computers with malware, banking trojans and RATs. There is an explosion of cybercrime – but just as with cyberspace, nobody knows exactly what the full scale of the problem is. Instead we have estimates and possibly biased statistics from a number of industry groups with vested interests in over-emphasizing up the problem. Without understanding the problem, there can be no solutions. The European Commission recognized this problem in 2007 when they issued a "general policy against cybercrime" noting that there was no agreed definition of cybercrime.[3]

The Commission's solution was to propose a threefold definition:
1. Traditional forms of crime such as fraud or forgery committed over electronic communication systems and information systems.
2. The publication of illegal content over electronic media (e.g. child sexual abuse material or incitement to racial hatred).
3. Crimes unique to electronic networks (e.g. attacks against information systems, denial of service and hacking).

3 European Commision. "Towards a general policy on the fight against cybercrime" May 2007

This threefold definition will prove useful in Chapter 3 (see page 19) with some restrictions. Certain cybercrimes are not profit motivated and it is hard to calculate the true costs of such crimes.

The difference in motivation is important. Although hacking is a cybercrime in itself, Gary McKinnon wasn't motivated by money when he broke into NASA's computers in 2005 – he was looking for evidence of the US government cover-up of aliens and UFOs. Likewise, when Anonymous hacked into the computer security company HBGary in 2011 and stole their email archives, their motivation was not money but to cause major embarrassment to that company. They accomplished this by publishing the data for everyone to see and not by selling it to the highest bidder or using cyber-extortion techniques. The methods behind the hacks remain the same – but the motivation behind the hackers varies. Hacktivists are motivated by a political agenda – or maybe just the fun and amusement – while cyber-criminals are all about abusing the internet for profit.

This helps us to answer the tricky question: What is cybercrime? For the purposes of this book, cybercrime can be characterized as the use of cyberspace by transnational criminal organizations whose sole motivation is theft.

In this way we can see that the cybercrime threat differs from traditional hacking, hacktivism, cyber-terrorism and cyber warfare simply because the threat level is so high. By focusing on profit-orientated cybercrime, we can exclude a large number of minor threats from the list. The ones that remain are the ones that make the headlines and have led to wild claims about the global cost of cybercrime. Although nobody can agree about the true costs of cybercrime, one thing is certain: cybercrime represents a real and present danger to the internet as cyber-criminals continue to infect computers with malware and steal with with little or no fear or retribution.

2

A NEW DARK ECONOMY

Cybercrime is a growth industry even in times of economic recession. The rapid expansion of the internet has fueled a massive increase in cybercrime across the internet. Early cybercrime was simple enough – hacking, virus writing, pornography, copyright violations and a small amount of credit card fraud. Now all that has changed: cyber-criminals have become the number one threat to the internet, and even the FBI are now making cybercrime their number one priority – relegating terrorism to second place. Between 2000 and 2009 the number of users on the internet grew from 394 million to over 1.858 billion. Wikipedia estimates that by 2013 around 39% of the world's population have access to the internet using computers or smartphones.

Most newbie internet users are not tech-savvy and know nothing about security. They unpack their computer, plug it into the phone line or Wi-Fi connection and connect to the internet. Their only chance of surviving a cyber attack is if the computer they own is updated automatically with anti-virus updates and patches to eliminate operating system vulnerabilities. Sometimes this does not happen. It has been calculated that the April 2014 obsolescence of the Windows XP operating system will leave millions without security updates. Net Applications, a US networking analysis company, have stated that 37.2 per cent of the computers connected to the internet are running Windows XP. If the Microsoft estimate of 1.4 billion computers running Windows operating systems is correct, then this means that an estimated 570 million computers will be vulnerable to new **zero day exploits** forever. The problem is worse in China than in the USA, where it is estimated that 72.1% of all the computers in China are running XP, as opposed to only 16.4% in the USA.

This rapid growth has left law enforcement playing catch-up. According to the Internet Crime Complaint Centre attached to the FBI, the overall cost of cybercrime to US companies has risen since 2001 from $17.1 million to an estimated $485.3 million. Some financial institutions and online banking sites never report cybercrime for fear that it will cause a loss of confidence in their security. On the other hand, security companies are alleged to "talk up" the statistics behind this type of cyber threat in order to sell more security software. The 2012 Norton cybercrime report claims that the costs of cybercrime are in the order of $110 billion per year, but estimates as high as this are at odds with other reports. Then again, figures as high as $1 trillion are bandied about by US government officials, though the source is another computer security company – in this case, McAfee.

When independent researchers are asked to evaluate the global cost of cybercrime, their figures are much lower. The Ponemon Institute surveys estimated the global costs as being $27 billion in 2012 and $34 billion in 2013. By contrast, the 2011 Detica report estimated the cost of cybercrime in the UK as £27 billion, while the 2012 report sponsored by the UK Ministry of Defence estimated that the direct costs of cybercrime were around £17 billion per year and that the indirect costs of cybercrime were around £5.8 billion. It turns out that nobody knows the true cost of cybercrime, a theme to which we shall return in Chapter 5, "The Hidden Costs of Cybercrime" (page 39).

Looking beyond the headlines – where anything related to the internet or computers automatically becomes a cybercrime in sensationalist press reports – there are a whole slew of potential crimes that can be committed using a computer and an internet link. High-profile hacking cases such as Gary McKinnon's, the online digital terrorism" of Anonymous and the antics of **LulzSec** are the tip of the cybercrime iceberg. Beyond the media headlines are the globally organized criminal gangs – who steal billions of dollars every year, with apparent impunity.

Who are the real cyber-criminals? If we ignore cybercrimes such as SPAM, intellectual property theft, cyber-stalking and cyber-bullying where the monetary cost is difficult if not impossible to quantify, and also the crimes that are committed via the internet but have a real world analog such as supplying illegal drugs or pornography, then we are left with the cybercrimes which actually steal money from people. Thus for the purposes of this book cyber-criminals are best described as transnational criminal organizations who use the internet and hacking techniques with the sole aim of monetary gain. This is an important point when examining the true cost of cybercrime. The same hacking tools and techniques are used by hacktivists, **white hat hackers** and cyber-criminals – but while cyber-criminals are motivated by a profit-based agenda and steal billions every year, the hacktivists are motivated by a political agenda, or sometimes just the fun and amusement or Lulz, while the white hat security industry just wants to profit off the cyber-criminals. Same tools. Same techniques. Different motivations.

Data-theft does not just lead to monetary loss. Hacktivists steal data and publish it for the world to see – devaluing the worth of the data to nothing. This is the hacktivist Art of Embarrassment: the art of data-theft to annoy and destroy. Hacktivists use online culture as a political forum by stealing and sharing data – but there is no use of the stolen data for financial theft. This is a major difference – cyber-criminals perform data-theft for money, hoarding stolen data and then selling it for profit. The aim of data-theft by cyber-criminals is to make money illegally. For cyber-criminals, the only point of data-theft is the misuse of stolen information to sell, trade or "cash out" the digital data for real, physical money. Cyber theft by profit-motivated cyber thieves is the number one problem of the World Wide Web. The huge costs of online theft by 2013 now means that cybercrime is the number one threat on the internet. Data theft by hacktivists is a rare occurrence, but profit motivated cybercrime is a constant threat.

The expansion of the use of computers and the internet to steal money has lead to an explosion of a New Dark Economy – but this growth has been matched by the increase of the Anti-Cybercrime Industry. The confluence of governmental and non-governmental cybercops with the traditional **computer security** industries has led to a deeper understanding of cyber-criminals. With the correct use of traditional search tools such as Google, novice cybercrime researchers can gather a wealth of interesting information, then build a Social Networking Analysis graph tracing the links between malware websites, online identities and hosting companies.

Such research is invaluable. Anyone with a reasonable knowledge of the internet – and a few advanced graphic visualization tools – can trace the activities of cyber-criminals and cyber-terrorists. Now anyone can be a cyber-vigilante.

The success of global co-operation has led to a large number of Digital Takedowns. Using false-front websites – **sting boards** – and false digital identities – **sock puppets** – the cyber cops have penetrated deeply into the online criminal subculture. The success of this approach can be seen in the 2012 sting Operation Card Shop – leading to 24 global arrests and the prevention of over $205 million (£131 million) in potential credit card fraud losses. As Operation Card Shop demonstrates, transnational co-operation between law enforcement agencies across the globe is the best way to fight the global cybercrime menace.

As the fight against cybercrime continues, cyber-criminals are performing hostile takeovers of millions of computers every year. The 2012 Norton cybercrime report claimed that there were 18 victims of cybercrime per second, but published no figures for malware infection, as opposed to **phishing** attacks, so it is difficult to calculate how many computers are infected with malware on a daily basis. This estimate might appear low, but when cyber-criminals try and infect the whole of the internet with crime-ware the chances of success are very high.

Once upon a time, cyber-criminals used targeted spam and phishingattacks to steal login credentials and other data through false-front websites that looked like the real thing. In the modern world, the same cyber-criminals hire black hat hackers to penetrate genuine websites – who then install software that infects ordinary users using zero day exploits. Once compromised the target computer downloads a RAT. Once your computer is infected with a RAT, it can steal your login IDs and passwords, your banking credentials, monitor your keystrokes and maybe even your physical actions, via your webcam. The use of simple hacking techniques has led to the exploitation and infection of millions of computers every year – an explosion of crime-ware-infected computers. This is the new face of cybercrime.

Cyber-criminals use crime-ware such as RATs to steal information – but there are different types of RATs. "Info-Trojans" exploit online social networking and email – stealing data and online credentials, then installing software without permission. But "Banking Trojans" such as **Zeus** steal money without you even being aware of it. The clever use of the Zeus banking trojan feeds you false data, lulling you into a false sense of security. Once the banking transfers are completed without the possibility of detection, it is already too late – your money has gone. If you are infected with a RAT, it is time to install some serious anti-crime-ware software – before your online digital identity is hijacked and used by cyber-criminals for illegal purposes.

Sometimes the data-thieves steal "nothing": the digital currency used in virtual worlds, the digital tokens used in multiplayer online role playing games, various digital certificates can all be "cashed out" in the real world via online auction houses such as eBay. Other times, online auction houses can be used for digital shoplifting. Real goods are purchased using fake Universal Product Code (UPC) barcodes, fake Radio-frequency Identification (RFID) tags and stolen credit cards used with stolen identities – and later "cashed out" for money. The growth in digital shoplifting and similar online frauds does nothing to inspire consumer confidence in the digital marketplace – undermining the growth of the online economy.

Once your computer is infected with a RAT, it can steal your login IDs and passwords, your banking credentials, monitor your keystrokes and maybe even your physical actions via your webcam.

The economic explosion of the Virtual Black Economy has been fuelled by the easiest and lowest entry level of cybercrimes – credit card fraud. Ever since there were Bulletin Board Systems, a small group of black hat hackers have specialized in credit card security with the sole motivation of profit through theft. The low entry level of credit card theft has spawned an entire digital online society, which uses criminal forums and secret Internet Relay Chat (IRC) channels to connect the buyer to a seller in a market where the article to be sold is stolen digital data. To service the Virtual Black Economy, a whole sub-industry has come into being – selling mag-stripe readers and writers, credit card data, foil printers, blank credit cards, fake holograms and hardware **skimmers**.

This form of "disorganized crime" is part of the "Digital Mafia", a hierarchy of online criminality controlled by untouchable cyber-criminal "Godfathers". Cybercrime starts with the underground digital Godfathers – who finance a whole slew of digital criminal enterprises – and ends with "cash out" mules that end up in prison. Either way, the only aim is to steal money.

Members of the Digital Mafia are the people who benefit most and have the least to lose in the cybercrime hierarchy. They can afford to invest their profits in a new crime-ware industry – the "Darkside Silicon Valley" of criminal malware programmers supplying the malware and crimeware programs that drive online financial theft. These highly organized digital criminals are behind the glut of malware on the internet. Crime-ware now comes "shrink-wrapped" with bug-fixes, technical support and bespoke malware customization. The rise of the Darkside Silicon Valley can be seen in the drop in prices. Every software industry is highly competitive and the crime-ware industry is no different. The Zeus Banking Trojan was originally $10,000 (£6,370) – but is currently available for around $500 (£318). The SpyEye Trojan was $4000 (£2,550) – but now only $600 (£382). The market is so overcrowded that some malware writers have made their crime-ware "open source" – giving it away for free.

> **Criminal black hat programmers are dedicated to only one thing: how to break into – and infect – as many computers as possible.**

Because of the explosion of the use of crime-ware on the internet, some security experts estimate that "every minute 232 computers are infected by malware". When malware is so easy to come by there is a plentiful supply of wannabe cyber-criminals. The entry level for sophisticated cybercrime is low and now requires little or no technical ability – attracting hoards of newbie cyber-criminals who want to steal your cash. Meanwhile the real money is falling into the pockets of the cyber-criminals who are vying to be the equivalent of a Darkside Microsoft – writing and selling crimeware for profit. Of course they "never get high on their own supply" by using their own product, which might attract attention from the cybercops. Instead they sell their crimeware into the food chain, and if anyone using it is caught they have guaranteed their anonymity in a number of ways.

The Digital Mafia behind these criminal software enterprises are often based in offshore hosting companies in what can only be described as digital gangster states, which have no extradition treaties and few cyber laws. These digital gangster states allow hosting of any content – for a price. **Bullet-proof hosting** guarantees that global legal agencies cannot shut down malware websites. Even when websites host infective malware, remote active trojans, phishing websites, or botnet control servers, the hosting sites refuse to shut down the offending websites. In some cases extradition is impossible – these countries refuse to sign the 2001 Budapest Convention on Cybercrime, allowing cyber-criminals in those countries to plunder computers across the world with little fear of legal retribution.

In January 2013 the US identified a Latvian named Denniss Calovskis as one of the programmers who wrote the Gozi banking trojan. The US government claimed that the malware infected over a million computers and was used to steal millions from the bank accounts of unwitting victims. When the US tried to extradite Calovskis to face trial, the Latvian government twice refused extradition requests. The Latvian foreign minister Edgars Rinkevics was quoted as saying that Latvian law guaranteed that people who broke the law suffered only "proportionate punishment" and that the possible prison term of 60 years which could be imposed by a US court was "amounted to an effective life sentence" and that it was "disproportionate to the amount" stolen. Finally, in August 2013, the Latvian government agreed to extradite Calovskis to the USA to stand trial. Calovskis denies all knowledge of the Gozi malware and in a statement claimed that "I don't know about the Gozi virus. I haven't helped any schemers to get money and I haven't received any." This case indicates the problems of prosecuting transnational cyber-criminals who use the internet for crime. Even if there is strong evidence linking a suspect to the creation of malware the problems of jurisdiction and differences in laws pertaining to cybercrime sometimes make prosecution difficult if not impossible.

The same cyber-criminals who form the Digital Mafia also fund Black Software Laboratories. Criminal black hat programmers are dedicated to only one thing: how to break into – and infect – as many computers as possible. Crime-ware research teams track their opponents from the computer security industry as actively as the computer security industry tracks cyber-criminals. Black hat programmers routinely reverse engineer security patches and virus updates for operating systems, then work backwards to find the security vulnerability – and then write a new exploit. With the majority of computers attached to the internet failing to update for up to three months – even after the issue of a security patch – it is inevitable that these cyber crooks will find a large number of computers to infect. This is the "fresh meat" of the modern online world that aids cybercrime to expand at an exponential rate.

Media headlines are full of sensationalized accounts of the digital super heists – the big hit that steals millions, or even billions, of dollars in a single robbery. Many of these crimes go unreported. Banking and financial companies rely on the confidence and trust of their customers, and are highly secretive about the true cost of cyber theft. Sometimes it becomes public knowledge – the big robbery of 42 million Rand ($4 million, £2.6 million) from Postbank in South Africa, the $10 million (£6.8 million) robbery of Royal Bank of Scotland (RBS) – but these are the tips of the iceberg. As we shall see in Chapter 5, "The Hidden Cost of Cybercrime" (page 39) the widely varying estimates of the costs of cybercrime by different organizations means that there are problems determining the annual cost of cybercrime.

Banking and financial companies rely on the confidence and trust of their customers, and are highly secretive about the true cost of cyber theft.

If the art of cybercrime is not getting caught, for cyber-criminals stealing "little yet often" is the best strategy. The Zeus Banking Trojan uses stolen banking credentials to steal small amounts of money whilst feeding false information back to the victim. The Koobface gang used social networking to entice victims to install unwanted software, they don't actually steal money from anybody, but these "salami slicing" tactics, which make only a few cents per install can make huge profits with little or no risk. The use of "Scareware" such as fake anti-virus is another good example of cyber-extortion and it appears that cyber-criminals who try to make "small profit from many people" have found a strategy that leads to low-risk, high-profit criminal activity. The use of "Scareware" such as fake anti-virus is another good example of cyber-extortion and it appears that cyber-criminals who try to make "small profit from many people" have found a strategy that leads to low-risk, high-profit criminal activity. The use of "scareware" and the growth of cyber-extortion are another example of low-risk profit based scams.

Stealing "less from more" is the number one cybercrime on the internet – and is growing exponentially. The transnational nature of these crimes and the small amounts stolen often mean that law enforcement agencies have neither the will nor the budget to investigate. These cybercrimes fly under the radar and attract little or no attention. Cyber cops prefer headline-grabbing digital takedowns involving million of dollars – because they lead to the justification of larger budgets. Meanwhile the minnows escape the net. More money is lost through small-scale cybercrime on a daily basis other than the true monetary losses of the few headline grabbing digital super heists.

But the cyber cops and other law enforcement agencies have not been idle. The use of forums and IRC by credit card fraudsters in an effort to remain anonymous has allowed the FBI and other organizations to penetrate their criminal enterprises. The use of digital informants – sock puppets – to lure cyber criminals onto fake cybercrime forums – sting boards – has led to global success. Once enough evidence has been harvested, the arrest teams move in. Digital takedowns are now frequent. If Operation Card Shop in 2012 was a major success it was partially due to the experience gained in other sting board operations. In 2008 the FBI shut down a ring of credit card cyber-criminals after penetrating an underground forum called "Dark Market". Similar operations using sting boards and sock puppets have allowed law enforcement to learn from their mistakes. The cyber cops are getting better every year. Soon there will be nowhere for cyber-criminals to hide – either online or offline.

If transnational cooperation is important between private cyber-security corporations and the cyber cops, how much responsibility for computer security lies with the average internet user? Worldwide co-operation in securing individual computers is very important. Securing your computer denies cyber-criminals access to the "easy pickings" they need to expand and grow. Security against cybercrime begins at home – and ends on the internet. Learn how to protect yourself … and your neighbors too. In the fight against cybercrime, local security is global security.

Cybercrime has many above-board costs but it is not just the cost of the cybercrimes themselves. Hidden costs are passed onto every citizen – whether they use the internet or not. The use of government, state and local tax monies to fund governmental anti-cybercrime task forces and police anti-cybercrime units costs money. The costs of upgrading and protecting banking and credit card security systems are directly and indirectly passed to every consumer. But maybe the largest hidden cost of the current online boom in cybercrime is the loss of faith in the security of online systems being used for communications, finance and commerce.

If cybercrime is undermining confidence in internet banking and online services – and thus slowing the expansion of the entire digital economy – then possibly billions could be lost due to the slow adoption of online commerce and finance. The billions lost through cybercrime – and the added billions spent in fighting cybercrime – might be tiny in comparison to the potential billions that could be gained in a world free from cybercrime. Cyber-criminals are damaging the expansion of the global digital economy – and perhaps that is the biggest cybercrime of all.

3

TYPES OF CYBERCRIME

How many types of cybercrime are there? It depends on which country you live in, as the laws vary. In countries such as Russia, which refuse to sign the 2001 Budapest Cybercrime Convention, there are few laws concerning cybercrime and so cybercrime flourishes. In countries such as the USA, law enforcement agencies such as the FBI have recognised nearly 100 different types and subtypes of cybercrime. Currently cybercrime is the number one priority of the FBI, even ahead of terrorism. Here is a list of the most common types of cybercrime.

Hacking: The Primal Cybercrime

Hacking is the archetype of all cybercrime. The hacking methods evolved by the hacking community over the last 30 years are used by every cyber-criminal. Without this knowledge developed by a generation of hackers, cyber-criminals would have no idea about how to hack into computers, take control of them and subsequently steal from their victims. But the early hackers were explorers in a new world, they had no idea that their ideas would lead to an explosion of illegal software designed to undermine trust in the web itself. In their innocence they opened a Pandora's box and designed many of the tools that are still used today. Hacking techniques, as listed below, lead to a whole host of crimes that are unique to the electronic systems that make up cyberspace – and facilitate cybercrime for profit.

Intrusion

The use of techniques to break into another computer, and take control. The intrusion techniques can be as primitive as guessing a password or as complicated as a cyber-criminal can make it. The use of zero day vulnerabilities combined with drive-by infection guarantees that no computer is safe. Any website can be compromised with the result that anyone who trusts that website can also be compromised.

Exploitation

Once the computer is compromised, the cyber-criminals can exploit your computer. They can download rootkits that hide their software. They can then download RATs, which can watch your every move. They can download other software that takes control of your computer and turn it into a zombie – part of a botnet of illegally hacked computers that are used by organized crime.

Hostile Takeover

Once a RAT or botnet client infects your computer, you no longer own your computer – somebody else does, who could be thousands of miles away. Your computer can be used to send spam, locate other computers to infect or participate in Distributed Denial of Service attacks – all in your name. When the FBI comes knocking on your door to ask you why you are sending death threats to the president, the chances are that somebody has hired an entire botnet to spam the government – and your computer was one of the infected.

Denial of Service (DDoS)

Many years ago, the best way to force a computer off the internet was to forge a series of TCP/IP packets using the Internet Control Message Protocol (ICMP) that said "the host is unreachable" – a subtle manipulation of the protocols that run the web. If an ICMP "nuke" was a sharp instrument, then modern-day techniques of DDoS are like a club. Given that most firewalls reject ICMP messages – including ping messages – cyber-criminals have come up with another solution: message flooding. By opening many channels with the target computer, by sending many packets at the same time, the target computer grinds to a halt. The use of botnets to amplify the DDoS attack over thousands, or hundreds of thousands of computers, makes things worse.

The Botnet Problem

Once upon a time on the internet, bots were remote attack tools used in the IRC wars of the early '90s, when hackers used to break in to computers, take them over and use them as if they were their own. Using another person's computer is a great way of hiding – some of the earliest proxy server programs in existence were crude hacking tools designed to mask the true IP address of the user. But some hackers went further, setting up bots that could be commanded to attack other users and computers from a remote destination. Once this idea was out in the open, other hackers modified malware and rootkit code to perform a hostile takeover of any vulnerable computer while being centrally controlled from a master server. The age of the "botnet" has arrived and the full ramifications of botnets are still to be felt across the internet. The current botnets are designed to facilitate cybercrime and the botnet clients are designed to steal user information, perform DDoS attacks and send spam. Even when a botnet is taken over, the core software of the botnet is designed for cybercrime, and until somebody designs a botnet that can be used solely for good, botnets will remain one of the major cyber threats of the modern world.

Internet Mediated Crimes

The knowledge and software used to penetrate system security was developed during the golden age of hackingnd has now been exploited by cyber-criminals. How? Because the internet is a facilitator; a medium of communication. True digital crimes over the internet are rare, but the growth of cybercrime that threatens the whole of the internet is becoming too common. The internet is the medium not the message, so attempts to blame the internet on the growth of cybercrime fall short of the mark. How many types of cybercrime are there?

There is a large group of cybercrimes that also exist in the real world. Drugs, porn, hookers and illegal material can be sourced from the internet, but also from a real world criminal. In this case the internet is nothing more than a facilitator that hooks up client with vendor. Services can be provided and money is made, but the internet is not instrumental in the crime. These are the traditional crimes that flourish on the internet.

Illegal Drugs

There are a large number of websites that can allegedly supply drugs that are illegal in some countries. These types of websites rely on word of mouth. In 2013 the FBI finally managed to locate the cyber-criminal behind the "dark web" drugs dealing website Silk Road It has been estimated that this underground website was facilitating an estimate $15 million in transactions annually.

Pharmaceutical Drugs

Viagra, Valium and other drugs only available by prescription are available on the web. Although illegal, the professionalism of some websites and the quality of the products they offer is such that they are seen as practical alternatives to conventional pharmacies.

Online Gambling

Gambling online is illegal in some places and not in others. Cyber-criminals use this fact to host offshore gambling operations accessible anywhere on the internet.

Online Pornography

Porn is legal in some places and not in others. Certain types of porn (child porn, animal porn and rape porn, for example) are illegal almost everywhere. The internet porn industry caters for all kinds but anyone who uses dark side websites should be warned that their credit card details could be stolen and they may be the subject to cyber extortion attempts.

Prostitution

Internet prostitution is big business. The use of online advertisements to advertise "single hookups" is big business. Internet-based call-girl services are big business. This would continue with or without the internet.

Indirect Cost Crimes

There is a large group of internet crimes whose cost cannot be measured directly. These crimes do not cause direct financial loss but damage possible sales, reputation and mental and psychological well-being...

Spam

Spam is unsolicited bulk email promoting or selling something, often illegal drugs, pornography and other illicit services. Originally automated programs via unprotected SMTP relays sent spam, but as the internet community secured their servers this became more difficult. In the internet of today, spam is mostly sent via botnets that are rented out by their owners, sending spam from hundreds or even thousands of compromised zombie computers. The Rustock botnet was a high volume botnet that from 2006 to 2011 had the capacity to send over 30 billion spam messages a day. When an operation involving the FBI, Microsoft and various security companies finally knocked Rustock offline, it was estimated that the global level of spam on the internet dropped by 27.4 per cent.[4]

The indirect cost of spam is the time needed to set up and maintain effective spam filters, and the time wasted reviewing email as possible spam. Since accepting email from known accounts only will defeat the

4 http://www.neowin.net/news/microsoft-took-down-rustock-botnet-thanks-to-67-year-old-counterfeit-law

purpose of email – to facilitate contact across the internet – time is wasted reviewing the spam folder for possible new contacts also.

Copyright Violation

It doesn't matter whether it is films, music or software, copyright violation has always been on the internet. Recent crackdowns on "file lockers" and torrent-sharing websites have had no effect. Data is infinitely replicable and every digital copy is the same as any other. Despite legal efforts, it is unlikely that copyright violation is going away very soon, and the use of blocking and throttling of torrent traffic by ISPs could have a harmful effect on the distribution of legal "open source" software and "creative copyright" music that is distributed free of charge.

Cyber-stalking

The use of modern internet technologies makes stalking easy. Social networks, webcams, GPS enabled phones and modern devices make cyber-stalking a known threat. In the modern world it is possible to purchase software to spy on a partner you suspect of cheating on you, but the uses of this software are not always legal.

Cyber Bullying

There have been several high-profile cases recently of the use of new technologies such as smart phones and social networking to intimidate people. The spreading of videos via YouTube, and the use of Twitter and Facebook posts, has caused suicides amongst the victims of cyber bullying. In 2013 a young girl of 14, Hannah Smith, commited suicide after enduring months of online bullying while using the social networking site Ask.fm.

Pay-per-install

On the darkside of the internet there are a lot of cyber-criminals who use pay-per-install to install unwanted software on the computers of victims such as adware, toolbars and so called "registry optimization software. Unlike with the scareware used for cyber-extorsion, the victims pay no money. Instead the time taken removing useless software and cleaning up their systems needs to be taken into consideration. There is a difference between the scheduled clean up of modern computers that we all need to do from time to time, and the loss of time and energy spent cleaning an infected computer. Software of this kind can also be a vector of infection for malware – a possible RAT or botnet client – hijacking your computer and using it to send spam or even be a part of a DDoS attack.

Direct Cost Crimes

These are the internet crimes where the cost can be measured in terms of the money which has been stolen from the victim.

Cyber Commerce

There is a huge and growing problem with online transactions for both buyers and sellers – a large amount never receive either the goods or the money. As users lose confidence in online commerce, there has been a huge increase in escrow fraud – where the seller lodges money with a bogus escrow agent only to lose their money and their goods. Online auction fraud is also a problem as stolen or counterfeit goods find their way onto the online market place. There are problems ascertaining the true value of the online economy and thus calculating the potential losses to digital commerce caused by lack of confidence is difficult, but it is almost certainly billion of dollars per year and some estimates place it higher.

Phishing

Phishing is "spam on steroids" – and is designed to entice the email recipient to access a certain website. Originally, phishing emails purported to be from a financial entity – a bank, credit card company or online transaction website such as PayPal or eBay – and directed the user to a website that looked exactly like the real thing. Once the user entered their credentials, these could be used by cyber-criminals for credit card fraud, or sold on to be used for identity theft. Modern phishing attacks often direct the victim to a website that has been compromised with malware, the victim then finds their computer compromised and a botnet client or RAT installed.

Cyber-extortion

Nobody knows the true monetary loss of cyber-extortion, because few victims report the crime. These internet blackmailers mostly target people who wander into the dark side of the web, people with something to hide. A recent spate of cyber-extortion targeted anyone who viewed a certain website, threatened them with the FBI, and asked them to pay a fine. Hackers have been known to steal credit card details and then offer to sell them back to the owners or place them on the internet. In 2011 IC3 reported that they had over 14,000 complaints of "FBI impersonation" scams.

Cyber Espionage

Industrial espionage has been around as long as there have been company secrets to steal, but the explosion of internet-connected devices has made it easier than ever. Techniques such as "Spear Phishing", where targeted emails within a single company allow the infection of entire corporate networks, are on the rise. Once inside the system, the cyber-criminals can steal company secrets, or new software under development, and any other proprietary information for financial gain.

Banking Theft

There is a new generation of RATs that do nothing but steal money. The current versions of the Zeus Trojan, or variants such as "KINS" or "Citadel" Trojans, install themselves on any vulnerable computer. Once installed they perform a full hostile takeover by intercepting banking details, stealing money from any available accounts and hiding themselves from infected users. Zeus not only steals money, it also masks the money transfers with phony information ensuring that the victim realizes the true scope of the theft only when the money is long gone.

Credit Card Fraud

The theft of credit card details is the number one problem on the internet. The issue is so great that the market for stolen credit card numbers has collapsed. New credit card details used for identity theft are now worth only a tenth of their original price. Your details might be available online for as little as fifty cents, a few pence or a couple of céntimos. If your details are stolen, they are available to the highest bidder. This criminal digital sub-culture of crowd-sourced credit card fraud is worthy of more examination. The use of the internet by disorganized crime provides an entire food chain of cyber-criminals with money, possibly costing the global economy millions of dollars every year. This problem is examined in more detail in Chapter 5 (see page 39), where the underground malware factories are examined in more detail.

Advance Fee Fraud

The so-called "Nigerian scam" (also called the "419 scam") works because people are both greedy and naive. Suppose you got a piece of spam from an alleged Nigerian prince or businessman offering you a lucrative opportunity of life. Would you really be naive enough to believe that out of all the people on the internet he chose you to help him… and be willing to share his fortune with you? Once hooked, the willing mark shells out money to facilitate banking transfers on the expectation of a financial pay-off, which of course never happens. People really do fall for this scam, even though it has been going for years.

27

Social Network Fraud

Do you really know everyone on your social networks? There has been a recent spate of "friend in trouble" scams across the social networks. The victim receives an email claiming to be from a friend travelling in a foreign country and in jeopardy – stolen passport, stolen money, medical problems, etc. – and asks for money to fly home. The unwitting victim sends money via one of the many services, only to find out their friend was fine all along.

Scareware Fraud

Scareware is a variation of pay-per-install using fake anti-virus software. A pop-up box appears on the victim's computer alleging that the computer is infected with a virus. The unwitting user then pays between $50 and $129 (£30–85) for a useless piece of software that does nothing. Sometimes that software is a virus – or worse, a RAT. In 2011, the FBI busted a group of online criminals selling fake anti-virus software, who are alleged to have made over $72 million (£46 million) with this scam.

Cybercrime is the big business of the modern digital age. New blackware companies write malware to subvert computers all over the internet. The new evolution of an entire black economy of malware threatens everybody. The chances of identity theft and online data-theft are growing every year. Now everybody is at risk of cyber threats from the new digital mafia. Everybody has to be vigilant. You must watch everything digital – your phone, your tablet, your laptop, they are nothing more than agents of cyber threat. Watch your computer! Don't let *it* watch you!

4

DARKSIDE SILICON VALLEY

We are living in an age where malware can be purchased "shrink-wrapped" on the cyber-criminal underground. This is malware designed for a single purpose to facilitate cybercrime and is purchased with a license and technical support just like ordinary software. The extraordinary growth of this industry has taken many experts by surprise. Unlike normal "hacker tools", which are distributed to a small circle of trusted friends, the new brands of crime-ware can be bought by anyone who has the money. This is very attractive to new cyber-criminals who have few, or little, technical skills. When you purchase the malware and technical support, your career in cybercrime can begin very quickly.

There are so many types of malware available on the internet, such as viruses, worms, **spyware**, adware, and rootkits, that to discuss them all would take a whole other book. But this chapter will focus on two types of malware that could best be described as "crimeware". These programs only exist to commit cybercrime. These are "crimeware" packages that allow cyber theft on a grand scale. They are the weapons for a new kind of crime that does not need to use violence. These are the sawn-off shotguns for a new digital age and cyber-criminals can steal more than any Brink's-Mat robbery, which managed to steal only $42 million (£26 million) of gold, diamonds and cash. In the Age of the web, digital money weighs nothing and is worth *much* more than its weight in gold when stolen. The new opportunities afforded by instant communication and instant connectivity are being used by cyber-criminals across the planet.

Exploit Kits

The first types of crime-ware to be discussed are **exploit kits**. An exploit kit is malware, which is a package of known exploits and zero day vulnerabilities. These exploit kits are designed to be installed on a malware hosting website. The website could be a legitimate, but compromised, website, or it could be a website inside known criminal domains hosted by bulletproof hosting companies. Once installed on a website, victims are enticed to visit the website through the normal vectors of cyber attack such as phishing. When the unsuspecting victim arrives at the website ,several things happen. Firstly, the malware detects the operating system type and which browser is installed. Then the malware selects an appropriate exploit from a range of possible exploits and uses it to compromise the computer by installing a "dropper". This dropper can then download further software such as a RAT.

This new breed of exploit kits allows anyone to install a large number of exploits, guaranteeing that a drive-by compromise will occur when the victim visits the infected website, but they are designed for easy use by the non-technical cyber-criminal. Although exploit kits use the computer vulnerabilities to probe and then exploit remote computers, the actual payload downloaded by the exploit is determined by the cyber-criminal who has configured the exploit kit. This allows exploit kits to be used for many different purposes – key logging, spam relaying, credential theft, adware installation, click-fraud and document theft are some of the most common.

Exploit kits typically include an administrator interface that provides detailed statistics to the cyber-criminals, including the number of visitors to the malware hosting site, which operating system and patch level the victim's computer is using, which web browser is being used, and most importantly, how many of the attempted exploits were successful. The statistical analysis is good enough to give a picture of which versions of which browser are most commonly used, along with detailed information about how much internet traffic is being redirected from the compromised or hosted malware referral sites, allowing the malware owners to tweak the software for optimal thieving efficiency.

The use of compromised legitimate sites enables drive-by infection, even if the victim is using a whitelist of allowed websites. This makes the whitelist approach useless in detecting and stopping such attacks; instead the user must rely on anti-virus, anti-spyware and other security software to block the threat. The use of zero day vulnerabilities means that many anti-malware packages will not have the correct signatures and thus not be able to detect the attack

Because it takes time between the discovery of a zero day exploit and the development of a detection signature, and it takes even longer for the vendor to determine the vulnerability and issue a patch, exploit kits are going to remain a threat for the near future – if not forever.

The "Eleonore" exploit kit first appeared in the middle of 2009. Since then, it has been continually upgraded and the current version is 3.1. It retails for an estimated $1200 (£750) in the underground black market and includes all the features of an advanced exploit pack, including older bugs that should have been patched years ago. The frequent upgrades, coupled with the addition of newer zero day exploits, indicates that the criminal software house writing this software is capturing and reverse engineering other malware to improve their own malware.

This new breed of exploit kits allows anyone to install a large number of exploits, guaranteeing that a drive-by compromise will occur when the victim visits the infected websites.

The "Phoenix" exploit kit is very similar to "Eleonore" and made its debut in 2010 at a cost of around $2000 and is currently upgraded to Version 3.1.15. It contains a larger list of exploits, but there is overlap between the two exploit kits in terms of the vulnerabilities exploited.

The "new kid on the block" is the "Blackhole" exploit kit. Currently at Version 2, Blackhole is available for around $500 per month to rent, along with a server to run the command and control software. If the cyber-criminal uses his or her own server, or a compromised server, then the price drops as low as $1500 per year. Technical support is available on weekdays from 9am until 7pm – showing that cyber-criminals work a normal working day. The authors of Blackhole have tried hard to obfuscate the malware code, making it more difficult for both security researchers and malware writers to reverse-engineer the code.

These exploit kits make it easy to package and maintain hosted or compromised websites and allow easy configuration of the malware to be installed. By using more than one exploit kit on a malware hosting server, the cyber-criminal increases the chance of success. If one of the exploit kits fails, there is a good chance that the other will succeed – a devastating double drive-by exploitation cyber attack. Exploit kits are becoming the number one menace on the internet and there are more than a dozen to choose from. When these exploit kits are combined with a payload such as the Zeus banking trojan (described below), exploit kits provide excellent return on investment for cyber-criminals.

The Zeus Banking Trojan

The Zeus banking trojan is currently running at Version 3.0 and it seems that it can be bought for $200–$500 on the black market. There a number of pirated copies available for download on cybercrime forums, but the evidence suggests that a large number of these copies are modified with further malware, allowing secondary theft from other cyber-criminals. Zeus is a RAT with botnet capabilities and cannot infect a computer on its own – it must be installed using a "dropper" and a known vulnerability. The combination of Zeus trojan and packaged exploit kits is dynamite. By using the zero day exploits as a dropper, cyber-criminals have managed to steal millions.

Unlike other RATs, Zeus is designed specifically for banking theft. The Zeus control interface allows the cyber-criminal to configure every detail within the trojan, and then package the malware using packing, obfuscation and encryption to evade current anti-malware signatures. Zeus is highly configurable, allowing targeted phishing attacks by country or by banking entity and thus increasing the success rate.

The command and control interface includes detailed statistical information on the Zeus banking operations, and allows the cyber-criminal to list the income generated by each "money mule" used to launder the money. Despite the fact that the Zeus banking trojan was first identified over three years ago, it is still popular and has spawned many variants. It has been estimated that Zeus has infected over 3.6 million computers in the US alone. Some security experts have estimated that the malware programming team responsible for the Zeus banking trojan are earning more than $800,000 per annum, but how much of this is profit is unknown, given the high outgoings when purchasing zero day vulnerabilities on the open market.

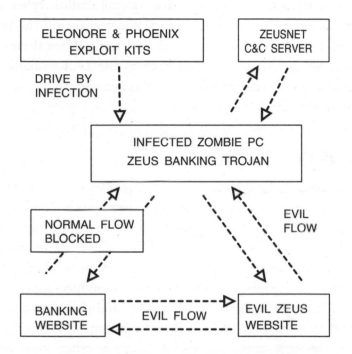

The use of exploit kits and the Zeus Trojan in action.

The diagram above shows the process involved in the exploitation and theft. Once the victim visits the infected website, one of the exploit kits will compromise the computer and download the dropper, which installs the Zeus trojan. When it's installed on the target computer the Zeus trojan uses a **man in the middle** attack to steal money directly from the bank account of the victim.

The following bullet points shows how Zeus works:

- The Zeus Trojan redirects all communication between the victim and a legitimate banking site through a compromised or "bulletproof" hosted site.

- The information flow between the bank website and the victim website can be recorded for later replay. The malware is capable of inserting bogus financial statements into the packet stream to socially engineer victims into believing that nothing is amiss, even after they have been robbed.
- The malware hosting website is capable of injecting custom JavaScript into the network connection in place of the real banking code. When the user executes the code, the Zeus trojan can then make seemingly genuine transfers while the user is still logged in and making other transactions.
- The credential theft module of the Zeus trojan means that even if the JavaScript injection method fails, the operators of the Zeus botnet can make transfers – for any amount, at any time.

In 2010 a cyber scam used these three pieces of shrink-wrapped malware to compromise the accounts of an estimated 3,000 customers of a UK-based online banking institution, stealing around £675,000 ($1.1 million) in a single cyber heist. In that same year the police arrested 19 people who used Zeus to steal an estimated $9.5 million ($15.4million). These attacks are just the tip of the iceberg and highlight just how attacks of this type are going to become a major threat to online banking in the future. The low cost for these crime-ware tools encourages more criminals to dabble in cybercrime. Maybe worse, these types of malware can be downloaded from many darkside websites and forums for zero cost.

Black Software Laboratories

There is a growth of underground black hat programming laboratories that are developing malware for sale to anyone who has the cash. These malware software writers are successful because they are copying the Silicon Valley model – anyone who buys their software can also purchase upgrades, technical support, bug-fixes and even bespoke customization of malware to suit any purpose.

Who will be the "darkside" Microsoft of the new digital dark age of cybercrime? There is evidence that cyber-criminals use the same techniques as computer security companies to capture, decompile, and modify malware. Malware is everywhere: possibly on *your* computer. If you can capture it, you can understand it. This is the key to understanding not only the computer security industry but also the Military Information Complex, and cyber-criminals.

Malware is computer code. Once captured and analyzed, it can be modified and replicated across the internet. Computer code is infinitely modifiable and infinitely replicable. Malware writers recycle their code and change it. This is to evade detection by anti-virus and anti-spyware software that relies on signature detection to block certain programs from executing. Malware writers use obfuscating techniques, which make it harder to analyze and recycle their code. One reason is to prevent analysis by anti-virus manufacturers and computer companies. The other reason is to prevent other cyber-criminals from decompiling, understanding, and recycling the malware.

This explains why there are so many "families" of malware and crime-ware that are highly similar. The cyber-criminals continually modify their

Simple modifications to a piece of malware can change the software signature significantly, meaning that an estimated 30 per cent of anti-spyware, anti-virus and anti-infection software fails to detect malware.

programs to escape the signature detection techniques of modern security software. Simple modifications to a piece of malware can change the software signature significantly, meaning that an estimated 30 per cent of anti-spyware, anti-virus and anti-infection software fails to detect malware downloaded off the internet. Part of the problem is the huge number of browser add-ons, extensions and modules that cannot be properly secured. The other part of the problem is that computer users often fail to upgrade their operating system or install security patches. A major issue is the huge number of Windows XP computers on the internet, and the lack of technical support and upgrades mean that these computers will be vulnerable forever. The major vector of cyber threat is not just in your computer operating system but also in the browser. It doesn't matter which internet browser you use – Internet Explorer, Firefox, or even Google Chrome –

because the plugins and add-ons to your browser which use common digital formats such as Word, Flash and PDF have all been under attack.

This is why "black ware" computer laboratories are so dangerous. They emulate the normal activities of software companies for evil purposes. They download and examine security patches issued by Microsoft and other companies. They examine, decompile and resurrect the exploit that the patch was designed to patch. Then they write their own exploit for the targeted system or add-on. They are evil programmers who write malware for money and they are a major threat to the integrity of the internet.

But, it gets worse. There is increasing evidence that malware programmers and black hat hackers are tracking the activities of the computer security industry and using those techniques. The use of **honeypots** to monitor hacker activity is well known in the security industry, and can also be used to capture malware code in the wild. The evidence suggests that the black malware laboratories are using the same techniques. By using honeypots, they can capture and decompile new malware as it appears. Once understood it can be modified, re-written and replicated across the entire internet.

This is the "dark digital mirror" of computer security; it is organized computer insecurity which emulates the computer security companies. They can, and do, track and observe high-profile vendors of operating system software, the programs, and their add-ons. The evil "blackware" laboratories ensure that nobody is safe, no matter what internet connected device they use, because botnets and RATs are starting to appear on all brands of smartphones.

The new breed of professional malware is a challenge to everyone because:

- It needs only a low level of computer expertise to attempt cyber-criminal activity. The abuse of the Silicon Valley model means that cybercrime toolkits come with technical support and software upgrades, allowing anyone with the cash to take advantage of the new digital dark-side economy.
- New software upgrades means that cyber-criminals can be in front of the traditionally reactive computer security industry. The black market in zero day vulnerabilities means that malware developers

will always be one step ahead of software developers and security experts.

- The new generation of malware is constantly responding to new anti-malware threats. Black hat researchers and programmers are running dark-side anti-security laboratories that mimic white hat security laboratories. They are constantly re-engineering their software to evade anti-malware security measures.
- There are no secrets within the malware community. Other malware laboratories run honey pots, capture malware and reverse-engineer it, then incorporate the newest features into their own breed of malware. Within days of the Stuxnet worm appearing, several other pieces of malware appeared using the same zero day vulnerabilities, indicating a high level of research and development on behalf of the malware programmers.
- It is possible to download this type of malware from almost anywhere on the web without paying. The malware software developers suffer just as much from piracy as Microsoft or other large software developers. It is possible to download cracked and pirated versions of almost every type of malware described in this book – but without the technical support or updates that a purchase and subscription would bring and with the near certainty that the pirates have modified the cybercrime code with a backdoor allowing them a full hostile takeover on a competing botnet.

The existence of underground malware laboratories has caused a glut of malware and crime-ware to flood the market. This has led to a fall in prices. Even with large number of cyber-criminals arriving on the internet every year, there is only a limited market for this type of malware. The high levels of competition have even led some malware programmers to quit the scene altogether, releasing the code of their malware as "open source" for anybody who wants to modify as they see fit. This has led to an explosion of new malware, which further saturates the market and forces prices down even further.

These new vectors of cyber attack are a constant threat to internet users. The evolution of RATs (designed for data and credential theft) into the Zeus banking Trojan (designed solely for online banking theft) is a major concern. There are already a number of Zeus variants available, and as more cyber-criminals study Zeus, with its sophisticated use of the man in the middle attack, these types of RATs will become more popular. After all, why bother stealing credit card details if you can get your hands on the cash directly? We are all living in a new age of cyber threat where the possibilities of cyber attack are multiplied by the existence of malware, which anyone can buy and use.

5

THE HIDDEN COSTS OF CYBERCRIME

What is the true cost of cybercrime? Nobody really knows the answer. We only have only surveys, guesses, predictions and extrapolations. In 2011 the UK Cabinet Office of Cyber Security and Information Assurance (OCSIA) worked with Detica, a subdivision of BAE, to produce a report looking at the cost of cybercrime in the UK. The Detica report estimated that the overall cost of cybercrime in the UK was £27 billion broken down as follows:

- The cost to UK citizens, through ID theft, online scams, and scareware, was estimated at £3.1 billion per year.
- The cost to the UK government caused by online fraud was estimated at £2.2 billion per year.
- The cost to UK businesses was estimated at £21 billion per year.

The bulk of the losses to UK business were attributed to two categories, intellectual property theft at £9.2 billion per year, and industrial espionage at £7.6 billion per year. As the report points out "with the exception of the well-understood and documented copyright theft issue, the types of IP most likely to be stolen by cyber-criminals are *ideas, designs, methodologies and trade secrets*, which exist mostly in tangible form and add considerable value to a competitor." However, it should be noted that IP theft and industrial espionage can be notoriously difficult to quantify in monetary terms. Even if it is noticed that the data has possibly been stolen, it may be impossible to know if the cyber-criminal uses the stolen intellectual property in such a way that it causes monetary loss to the victim.

If we scale the figures given by the Detica report to a global level, assuming that the UK has 5% of global GDP, then we get a figure of £540 billion, a figure which is ridiculously large even by the worst estimates of computer security companies. If we exclude the figures for IP theft and industrial espionage, then the annual cost of cybercrime in the UK falls to approximately £7.6 billion, which scales to a global loss from cybercrime as £93.1 billion, which is much closer to some recent security industry estimates.

There have been various estimates for the cost of cybercrime in 2012. The Ponemon Institute produced the following figures based on a survey of US companies and concluded that the annual cost of cybercrime in the US was $8.9 million per year. It should be noted that this sample is highly self-selecting. Out of 683 US corporations that were asked to participate in the survey, 76 initially agreed, but only 56 finally took part. As we can see from the table below, the estimated total global losses from cybercrime were a mere $26.7 million.

2012 Ponemon Report

Country	Total in US$
US	$8,933,510
UK	$3,252,912
Australia	$3,386,201
Germany	$5,950,725
Japan	$5,154,447
Total	$26,677,795

Source: "2012 Cost of Cybercrime Study: United States", 2012, Ponemon Institute

Security industry estimates tend to be a lot higher. The 2012 Norton cybercrime report estimated that global losses through cybercrime were $110 billion (£68 billion). The losses total an average of $197 (£120) per individual across the world. According to the report an estimated 1.5 million people become victims of cybercrime every day, and a total of 556 million victims per year. In the cybercrime world, there are 18 victims per second.

The Internet Crime Complaint Centre, attached to the FBI, estimated that the cost of cybercrime in the USA was $525 million in 2012. Conventional wisdom indicates that the USA have approximately 25 per cent of the global GDP, and scaling this figure up gives us an estimate of roughly $2.1 billion for global cybercrime costs.

A figure of $1 trillion annual[5] losses is often quoted by US government officials such as General Keith Alexander, the director of the **NSA**, but this is almost certainly a gross overestimate. Even the security experts who contributed to the 2009 McAfee report have expressed dismay at the way the numbers have been extrapolated. As Ross Anderson, a security engineering professor at Cambridge University, commented "the intellectual quality of this ($1 trillion number) is below abysmal."

What we do know is that the trend is upwards. The 2013 Ponemon Institute study of cybercrime can be contrasted with the 2012 report. In 2012 the total global cost of cybercrime across the organisations surveyed was $27 million, but by 2013 the figure was $34 million. We are swimming in data and statistics, but we are no closer to knowing the true cost of cybercrime.

Does cybercrime really have such an impact on global wealth? Are the statistics manipulated to facilitate a whole new computer security economy, while providing governments and law enforcement agencies with justifications for larger budgets? Or, perhaps it's true as the saying goes, that "99 per cent of all statistics are made up".

But why is this a problem? We need to understand the true costs of cybercrime. It is important to calculate the true cost of cybercrime in order to evaluate the current level of risk. Users need to balance their need for security against the cost of pro-active security software, such as anti-virus, firewall and anti-malware software. Industry and corporations need to understand the true extent of the problem to protect their systems

5 Peter Maass & Megha Rajagopalan, "Does Cybercrime Really Cost $1 Trillion?", 2012, ProPublica

and apply appropriate computer security techniques. Finally, governments need to evaluate the costs of cybercrime to facilitate the formation of governmental policy, laws and budgets for cyber-security. Without such policies, the problem of cybercrime cannot be debated on a global scale, and it will be impossible for transnational law enforcement agencies to cooperate if there are no treaties and agreements in place.

Without an accurate estimate of the scale of the problem, it is impossible to have a logical debate about the huge impact of cybercrime within our digital society.

We need to go beyond the hype of the computer security vendors and of government and law enforcement. To understand the evil nature of the impact of cybercrime on our society and our society and civilization, we need to see how deep the rabbit hole goes. We need to ask a key question:

Why do these estimates of the costs of cybercrime vary so much?

The answer is simple: the nature of cybercrime surveys is highly flawed and there are several problems that need to be addressed when evaluating the true cost of cybercrime.

Under Reporting

Various organizations such as banks and online financial entities like to play down the risks of cybercrime. This is to ensure that there is no loss of confidence in the organizations involved. It has been alleged on several occasions that large banks have lost millions in cybercrime heists, but many of these banks reply to questions with a "No comment".

Over Reporting

Other organizations such as computer security companies and law enforcement have been accused of talking up the threat. The reasons are obvious. On the one hand, vendors of computer security products are going to sell more of their products if they can engender a "climate of fear". On the other hand, law enforcement can apply for bigger budgets to tackle the cybercrime menace, and expand their anti-cybercrime operations.

Self Reporting

Unlike normal statistical surveys that try and sample a representative portion of the population, cybercrime statistics are reported by the victims. This is not a representative sample of the victims of cybercrime. Some victims might not realize that they have been robbed, other victims might, for whatever reason (e.g. porn scams), chose not to report the crime. The "Koobface" gang earned millions using "pay-per-install" techniques, but it is hard to define exactly what was stolen from the victims.

However, the 2011 report from Microsoft Research entitled "Sex, Lies and Cybercrime Surveys" examined previous cybercrime surveys and arrived at the conclusion that there is a statistical bias that inflates the estimates of the costs of cybercrime. Although the statistics are the key to understanding the problem, they are beyond the scope of this book, and the statistically minded reader should read the report in full.

Some victims might not realize that they have been robbed, other victims might, for whatever reason (e.g. porn scams), choose not to report the crime.

The report begins by examining the problems of surveys of sexual behavior and looks at an obvious paradox. The statistics show that men report having more female sexual partners than the females report having male sexual partners. This is, quite obviously, impossible. So why is there such a huge discrepancy in the two figures?

The answer is simple: If only a very small proportion of the men surveyed report having large numbers of sexual partners e.g. 100 or 200 partners in a lifetime, then this inflates the statistics. If a male respondent claims to have had 100 sexual partners, when the real figure is the average of 20, this adds a huge response error to the statistics. When the male respondents who make extreme claims about sexual partners are removed from the data set, the figures for male and female sexual partners begin to match up. Suddenly the statistics start to make sense.

Why is this important in evaluating the truth of cybercrime surveys? Because cybercrime surveys suffer from exactly the same problems as sex-based surveys. They rely on self-reporting, so it is possible that a few respondents who over-estimate their losses from cybercrime can skew the statistics of the survey, making it appear that the losses from cybercrime are far greater than they are in reality.

As the report points out, when errors like this creep into a survey with 1000 respondents, each dollar of claimed losses translates into an extra $200,000 dollars on the total estimate. A victim who claims $50,000 in losses adds $10 billion to the statistics, five such respondents add over $50 billion to the alleged cybercrime losses. The report concludes that the current cybercrime surveys, where 75 per cent of the estimated losses come from the reported answers of just one or two people, are unreliable. Once again, the statistics start to make sense.

Using these insights, a team of computer security experts was commissioned by the UK Ministry of Defence in 2012 to analyze the "true cost" of cybercrime, and they came to conclusions which impact society as a whole. The report begins by defining where losses occur when cybercrime is committed.

Direct Losses

This is where the money or its equivalent is lost. It is the direct consequence of cybercrime and the impact on the victim.

- Money withdrawn from the victim's account.
- Time to reset banking credentials for both banks and consumers.
- Distress suffered by victims.
- Secondary cost of overdrawn accounts e.g. no access to money, unpaid bills.
- Lost attention and bandwidth caused by spam.

Cybercrime: Direct Costs

Online banking fraud (phishing)	$320m (£200m)
Online banking fraud (malware consumer)	$70m (£44m)
Online banking fraud (malware business)	$300m (£188m)
Fake anti-virus	$97m (£61m)
Copyright (software)	$22m (£14m)
Copyright (media)	$150m (£94m)
Pharmaceuticals	$288m (£180m)
Stranded traveller scam	$10m (£6m)
Fake escrow scam	$200m (£125m)
Advance fee fraud	$1,000m (£625m)
PABX fraud	$4,960 (£3100m)
Online card fraud	$4,200m (£2625m)
Offline card fraud (domestic)	$2,100m (£1312m)
Offline card fraud (international)	$2,940m (£1837m)
Total	$16,657m (£10409m)

Source: Cybercrime: Estimated Global Direct Costs, provided by Anderson et. al. (2012).

Cybercrime: Indirect Losses

These are the losses across the entire digital community when cybercrimes are committed, whether they are successful, or not.

- Loss of trust in online banking, leading to a drop in revenue for online banks.
- Missed business opportunities for banks to use email to communicate with customers.
- Reduced uptake of electronic services because of the reduction of trust in online services.

Cybercrime: Indirect Costs

Loss of confidence (consumers)	$10,000m (£6,250m)
Loss of confidence (business)	$20,000m (£12,498m)
Clean-up costs (ISPs)	$40m (£25m)
Clean-up costs (Users)	$10,000m (£6,250m)
Total	$40,040m (£25,021m)

Defence Costs

These are the types of proactive measures that are designed to prevent cybercrime from being committed.

1. Security products such as spam filters, anti-malware and anti-phishing toolbars.
2. Security services such as training and computer security awareness measures.
3. Security services to industry, such as website "take down" services.
4. Fraud detection, tracking and recuperation of stolen money.
5. Law enforcement.
6. The inconvenience of missing an email message falsely classified as spam.

Cybercrime: Defence Costs

Banking technology countermeasures	$1,000m
Banking & Merchant costs	$2,400m
Anti-virus	$3,400m
Cost of "patching" security holes	$1,000m
General computer security	$1,0000m
Law enforcement	$400m
Total	$18,200m

We are now in a position to calculate the "hidden cost of cybercrime", the true impact on society that the flourishing cybercrime community costs our global civilization every year.

Hidden Costs of Cybercrime

Defence Costs	$18,200m
Indirect Costs	$40,040m
Total	$58,240m

Source: Ross Anderson, Chris Barton, Rainer Bohme, Richard Clayton, Michel J.G. van Eeten, Michael Levi, Tyler Moore & Stefan Savage, "Measuring the Cost of Cybercrime", 2012

The hidden cost of cybercrime and its impact on society can only be only be measured by the cost of cybercrime when compared to other offenses. When compared against other types of crime such as War on Terrorism and War on Drugs, it soon becomes obvious that (i) more is spent on preventing cybercrime than cybercrime actually costs, and that (ii) the indirect costs of cybercrime are higher than the costs of cybercrime itself. This is an astonishing finding that has a huge impact on policy development.

When you consider that the 2011 McKinsey Global Institute report estimated that the true value of the global internet economy was worth $8 trillion, and that between 15 per to 36 per cent of all internet users refuse to use online financial services due to a lack of confidence in internet services , then we can clearly see that cybercrime is not only stealing wealth, but it is preventing online wealth generation. Cyber-criminals are not just stealing from our pockets, but from the pockets of our children who will never benefit from the growth of online services that might have been.

The 2012 report by Anderson et al which was prepared by request of the MoD as a response to the report by Detica in 2011 comes to a conclusion that in this author's view is entirely correct: "We should spend less in anticipation of cybercrime (on anti-virus, firewalls etc.) and more in response, that is on the prosaic business of hunting down cyber-criminals and throwing them in jail".

Conclusion

The threat of cybercrime goes far beyond the actual losses of cybercrime. The pro-active use of anti-virus and other anti-malware software does nothing to ameliorate the vectors of cyber attack.

Modern techniques of signature detection in anti-malware products are useless in the modern world – the expenditure for anti-malware and anti-virus products far outweighs the risk and the cost of cybercrime.

There is only one conclusion, as the 2012 Anderson report rightly says, we need to spend more on law enforcement and less on anti malware software – which doesn't work in many cases against zero day vulnerabilities and morphic malware signatures anyway. As we know from our experiences in the modern world of cyber threat, malware programmers from the "dark side" of the internet can mutate, change, modify and adapt computer code for their own purposes.

So, how do we combat cybercrime? The conclusion: we must use every means necessary to improve the internet. The 2006 Aaron Emigh report sponsored by the Department of Homeland Security on the "crime-ware landscape"[6] came to similar conclusions as the UK's Ministry of Defence report of 2012. So, while still using conventional protection such as firewalls, anti-malware software and code execution monitoring software, we should attack crime-ware at its source. Their countermeasures include:

1. Interfere with the distribution of crime-ware via filtering, automated patching and countermeasures against content injection attacks. Spam filters can prevent the delivery of deceptive messages. Automated patching can make systems less vulnerable. Improved countermeasures to content injection attacks can prevent cross-site scripting and SQL injection attacks.
2. Prevent infection of the computing platform with protected applications. Signature-based anti-virus schemes have problems with reaction time to new attacks, with highly polymorphic code,

6 "The Crime-ware Landscape: Malware, Phishing, Identity Theft and Beyond", Dept. Homeland Security, 2006

and with rootkits that obscure crime-ware. Behavioural systems can react immediately to new attacks, but false positives are a serious problem, as consumers are unwilling to tolerate interference with legitimate code. Protected applications that cannot be overwritten or patched except with certified code hold the promise to prevent infection of existing applications and system files.

3. Prevent the crime-ware from executing by validating code prior to execution. A low-level mechanism ensuring that only certified code can execute could help prevent attacks, but may prove too restrictive for users, who may have legitimate reasons to run uncertified code.

4. Prevent the removal of confidential data from storage by restricting access to confidential information by unauthorized code at the hardware level. The ability to prevent rogue code from accessing confidential data would be highly useful in preventing access to especially sensitive data, such as signing keys. Specialized hardware is generally required to provide such an assurance.

5. Prevent the user from providing confidential information by monitoring keystrokes and/or providing a hardware-level trusted path from the keyboard, and storing keyboard-avoiding credentials securely. Some forms of "white hat key-loggers" can detect when a user is providing credentials to a site that should not receive them. User interfaces need to be vetted to ensure that users can readily provide data to an intended data recipient, while the entry and transmission of data to an attacker are effectively impeded. A hardware-level trusted path could ensure that keyboard data is appropriately encrypted for the intended data recipient before an attacker could obtain keystrokes. Securely stored credentials can obviate the need for keystrokes in many cases.

6. Interfere with the ability of the attacker to receive and use confidential data by encoding data in a form that renders it valueless to an attacker. Some products sniff traffic to detect a compromise of confidential data. Content-based schemes are suitable for detecting inadvertent compromises, but can be readily overcome by crime-ware that employs encryption. Code execution prevention based on

behaviour-based systems[77] hold promise, but cannot detect all fraudulent use, and false positives remain an issue. An effective countermeasure at this step is to ensure that data is encoded in a form that renders it valueless to an attacker. Examples of such encodings include encryption that is inextricably bound to a particular communications channel with an authenticated party, and public-key encryption of data that incorporates strict limitations on its use.

All of this leads to the conclusion that the best way to protect the internet from the scourge of cybercrime is to adopt a policy that mirrors military strategy: deny, degrade and destroy.

Deny

Deny the cyber-criminals access to your computer. Security starts at home. Taking steps to secure your computer by regularly updating with security patches helps. Installing anti-malware and a firewall on your computer helps. By denying the low-hanging fruit of an unsecured computer to cyber-criminals – who could be anywhere in the world – your actions make the internet safer. The use of common security programs is not a 100 per cent guarantee that your computer will not be infected. Denying cyber-criminals access is not just about installing the latest software fixes for your computer. The most modern vectors of cyber attack are psychological "social engineering" attacks: spam, phishing, and spear phishing. If you upgrade your brain, and not your computer, cyber-criminals who use those attacks will fail every time.

Degrade

Degrading the support network used by cyber-criminals makes it harder to find new victims. There are so many botnets on the internet that it is

7 It is possible that behaviour-based systems that prevent malware code from executing can prevent access to files that appear to contain malware. When programming computer code, the system cannot tell the difference between a programming error and a malware attack and will quarantine faulty code as if it was malware, much to the frustration of the programmer.

difficult to destroy them all. Their persistence and long term use of rootkits make them hidden to the majority of users. The "Conficker" worm is alleged to be installed across the internet, and many experts believe that "Conficker" is a latent trojan horse that can be awakened any time to do more digital internet evil.

The modern use by security experts to locate, monitor and destroy the command and control servers used by botnet herders degrades the capacity of cyber-criminals to mount their attacks. Operations against botnets make the internet safer. It was estimated that the destruction of the "Rustock" botnet in 2009 caused a 30 per cent drop in global spam volume, thereby degrading the capacity of cyber-criminals to send spam and phishing emails. The FBI uses cyberspace to catch cyber-criminals. The use of sting boards and other methods degrades the confidence of cyber-criminals in their alleged partners in crime. This is the use of "Digital COINTELPRO" to infiltrate, gather intelligence, and then arrest the perpetrators. The online FBI agents like Master Splntyr are the new agents of destruction for the digital online cybercrime communities.

Destroy

Although cybercrime community is a transnational digital mafia, law enforcement is making inroads into the cybercrime community – with great results. The lack of any international agreements about what constitutes cybercrime hinders law enforcement, over and above any normal problems of global cooperation. The problem of destroying cybercrime transcends normal law enforcement and enters the political zone because the problems of the lack of transnational cooperation can be resolved only at that level, with agreements between governments and the need for possible UN treaties.

Tougher legislation that allows law enforcement to follow the money across borders would enable the destruction of many cyber gangs. If it is harder to cash out, then cybercrime will not pay.

Finally, the problem of gangster states that permit cybercrime to flourish within their borders must be resolved. It has been suggested by the UK's *Daily Telegraph* that Russia is a gangster state because " a state without constraints becomes a gangster", but maybe that is too simplistic.

Misha Glenny (2008) described gangster states as a "corruptocracy"[8]. They are nations of "drugs and thugs" where the "triangle of crime, business and politics" applied "corruption as an ideology". If Russia would not only sign the 2001 Budapest Convention on Cybercrime but also enforce it, then many of the malware hosting websites would vanish from the internet, spam and phishing attacks would decrease and cyber-criminals would suffer a terrible blow. There should be no nation which allows, and maybe encourages, cyber-criminals to flourish inside its border, unless they are using them as proxy agents in the current cyberwars.

Where are the "Digital Gangbusters" against cybercrime syndicates now? We all are. If we want to protect the internet we need to destroy cybercrime before it further dominates the internet. This is the age of the digital neighborhood watch, where security at home makes sense. We should track down, arrest and prosecute cyber-criminals and, if possible, send them to jail. They undermine the internet. They are destroying the growth of the cyber-economy. They must be stopped. Now it is up to you.

8 Misha Glenny, "McMafia: A Journey Through the Global Criminal Underworld", 2008

6

DARK WEB

Do not mistake the "deep web" with the "dark web". The "deep web", or "invisible web", is a legitimate use of the world wide web. There are online websites which cannot be indexed because (a) the "spiders" that crawl the web obey the "robots.txt" file, which politely asks a crawler not to read parts of the website; (b) the pages delivered to the web browser are generated dynamically using scripts and databases on the web server and there are no static HTML pages to be retrieved; or (c) the website is password protected. Of course it is possible to (a) ignore the "robots.txt" file and retrieve everything on the website, or (b) write programs that crawl through the dynamically generated page and then post-process the output to access the information which would be shown in the web browser, or even (c) use hacking techniques to gain access to the web server content directly.

However, this is both ethically dubious or costly in computational terms. Some online companies use techniques to discourage the spidering of their websites and prevent the copying of dynamically generated information. Internet users with no home connection, who download websites for later reading at home using software such as Teleport Pro or HTTTrack, will have encountered this problem. Some websites are designed not to be downloaded and used offline. The deep web is a mystery only because it doesn't appear in the search results of major search engines such as Google or Bing, but the deep web is accessed by billions of users everyday through social networking sites such as Facebook and the myriad of community forums. Sites such as Facebook which protect their intellectual property by not being indexed are a large part of the deep web. Indeed, being a part of the deep web guarantees that the user navigates through the entire site rather than jumping to the page of interest increasing the chance of seeing a relevant advertisement and thus profits.

The dark web or darknet is a different animal entirely. The dark web is designed to piggy-back on the normal protocols used by the internet and provide 100% anonymity for the users. If you don't install the software used by the dark web, you will never find it as an ordinary user. The commonest method of accessing the dark web is to install the Tor anonymity package, which allows near perfect anonymity for Tor users. Originally developed in 2002 by the US Naval Research Laboratory, Tor was designed to allow totally anonymous communications across the internet for government agencies, but it has been adopted by the internet community at large as well as dissidents and activists in countries such as China who wish to remain anonymous in a country where internet access is tightly controlled and censored.

Tor has recently been colonized by more than just activists and cyber-hacktivists. The network has been widely used by cyber-criminals who provide pornography, drugs and guns on the dark web. In 2013 the FBI finally managed to locate the cyber-criminal behind the dark web website Silk Road which specialised in selling anything illegal. It has been alleged by law enforcement agencies that Silk Road was one of the largest illegal trading websites on the dark web. By trading in illegal drugs, prescription pharmaceuticals, fake ID cards and even weapons, it appears that Silk Road was a major player in the cyber-crime arena. It has been estimated that this underground website was facilitating an estimate $15 million in transactions annually. When the alleged owner of the website Ross William Ulbricht (a.k.a Dread Pirate Roberts) was finally arrested, the FBI seized around $3.6 million dollars in the digital currency known as Bitcoin. Meanwhile other cyber-criminals have not been idle to find opportunity in the collapse of Silk Road, and within weeks a number of competing websites emerged on the dark web claiming to be Silk Road 2.0. The current list of dark web sites available from online sources on the internet reads like a cyber-crime hall of fame, with child pornography, drugs, guns, false documents and blank credit cards at the top of the list. The dark web has been colonized by cyber-criminals while nobody was looking.

What can law enforcement do about cyber-crime on the dark web? According to the reports from the FBI, there is no possibility that the Tor network itself has been compromised; they insist that the perpetrator failed to take basic cyber-security steps to protect himself when logging on, and that a name found inside an email was the final evidence that brought down Silk Road. But is that true? We already know from the documents leaked by Edward Snowden in 2013 that the NSA and GCHQ have for some time now been seeking methods of breaking into the Tor network as used by cyber-criminals and -terrorists. When the US government funded the Tor project, they designed the software to be virtually unbreakable. It could be argued that they did too good a job, and now that Tor is being used for constructing the dark web they find themselves in the unenviable position of trying to hack into the Tor network for intelligence-gathering purposes. The 2013 documents provide evidence that a joint effort by the NSA and GCHQ called "Egotistical Giraffe" is trying to find methods of subverting and undermining the Tor protocols in the name of the War on Terror. The problem, though, is that there are activists, journalists and dissidents who are breaking no laws in the Western nations, but who could be in serious danger in their own countries if the Tor network was compromised.

There are very few places where our electronic communications are guaranteed protection and privacy from the efforts of NSA and GCHQ surveillance programs such as PRISM, and the Tor network is one of them. We are approaching a digital two-tier society where only certain nation states, large corporations, and intelligence agencies can afford the luxury of the expectation of privacy in electronic communications. Ordinary internet users might as well send a carbon copy of every email, a tape recording of every phone call and a photocopy of every letter and invoice to the NSA and GCHQ, because privacy is a luxury that has been taken away from us without us even realizing it.

SECTION TWO

CYBERWAR

"We'll see cyberwar in our lifetime..."

Mellissa Hathaway,
US Governnment cyber-security expert

Cyberwar is a global information warfare waged across the internet, acted out by cyber-warriors, cyber-terrorists and cyber-hacktivists backed by nation states. Cyber weapons are being developed by over 100 different countries and we are in the middle of a a cyber arms race.

7

DIGITAL COVERT WARFARE

Understanding the true nature of modern digital covert warfare is easy; it is just like traditional covert warfare. Spying and the art of espionage have been used in warfare throughout history, but one of the first books to lay out a blueprint for covert warfare was *The Prince*, written by Machiavelli (1469–1527) circa 1513 but not printed until 1532, five years after his death. These ideas were refined and honed during the centuries of war between European states and became the foundations for modern espionage.

By the Middle Ages England had already developed an extensive network of spies, which reported to Queen Elizabeth I. Her spymaster Francis Walsingham (1532–1590) ran a network of spies which was responsible for gathering the evidence that condemned Mary Queen of Scots to death by beheading. It is rumoured that Baden Powell, the founder of the Boy Scout movement, was a spy during the Boer war and that he disguised the layouts of forts in pictures of butterflies. In the period between 1900 and 1925 Sidney Reilly (1873–1925), the Ace of Spies was a quadruple agent, who worked for the UK, Germany, Japan and the Russian Czar, and it has been claimed that he was the inspiration for the fictional spy James Bond. The most infamous spy of World War I was Margaretha Geertruida Zelle, better known as Mata Hari, who was convicted of spying for the Germans and was executed by firing squad in 1917.

The finest expression of covert warfare was during the Cold War as spies from the eastern and western blocs fought a secret war using modern espionage techniques. The normal spying methods of the cold war spies included espionage, subversion, surveillance, psychological operations (PSYOPS), counter-intelligence programs (COINTELPRO) and sabotage. Infiltrators, who came to be called "moles", joined intelligence agencies while secretly working for and passing information to the USSR.

In the UK one of the most famous cases was the Cambridge Five, a group of students who were recruited by the communists in the 1930s, successfully penetrated UK intelligence agencies and subsequently passed secrets to the USSR. Guy Burgess (1911–1963) and Donald Maclean (1913–1983) were both members of the intelligence community who spied for the USSR during the Second World War and the early Cold War. They went off the grid in 1951 and eventually defected to Russia around 1956. Burgess and Maclean were warned by Kim Philby (1912–1988), another double agent who worked for British intelligence and the USSR, and who defected in 1963. Anthony Blunt (1907–1983), a respected art historian with establishment links, was exposed as a double agent in 1979 and subsequently stripped of his knighthood, while John Cairncross (1913–1963) was unmasked as a spy twice – firstly by the intelligence community in 1951, and finally in 1990 to the general public.

So if espionage has a long history, what has changed? The development of the internet and the growth of cyberspace have enabled the intelligence community to use the internet as a vehicle for espionage, surveillance and possibly even sabotage. This use of the internet as a force multiplier by the intelligence community makes the new age of modern digital warfare more dangerous than anything we have seen to date. In the digital age any of these covert operations can take place anywhere across the web. The roots of modern cyberwar and the current covert digital wars raging around the globe can be found within history. The motivations of traditional spy craft remain the same, but now the battle-space is the internet and traditional "tradecraft" has been updated for the modern digital age.

Espionage

Spying and the art of uncovering hidden secrets is the key piece of this jigsaw. Throughout history leaders have tried to lift the fog of war and dominate the **battle space** through knowledge of their opponents' forces dispositions and intentions. Sometimes the knowledge gained by espionage is the key turning point in a war or battle – the cracking of the Nazi codes by code breakers at Bletchley Park or the US decoding of the Japanese naval codes, both during the Second World War, are excellent examples of this. In the modern world, digital codes are exponentially more sophisticated but as we shall see later in this chapter possibly not good enough. There is growing evidence that even the most sophisticated of codes used by internet users on a daily basis are easily broken by the NSA, and that even if you encrypt your email you might as well write it on a postcard and mail it to them directly. The 2013 PRISM revelations by Edward Snowden have given us a unique insight into the digital espionage programs that currently exist in the USA and this is dealt with in more detail in Chapter 17 (page 162). The evidence suggests that the cyberwar with China is based largely on espionage. Operation Aurora spied on US high-technology firms such as Google, Operation GhostNet used RATs to spy on opposition groups attached to the Dalai Lama, while Operation ShadowNet used a botnet to target Indian strategic and diplomatic interests. All of these cyber-espionage operations have close links to Chinese military and political interests and it has been concluded that the Chinese have advanced cyber warfare and cyber-espionage capabilities. It appears that Chinese cyber warfare espionage techniques using RATs are an **Advanced Persistent Threat** (APT). While some cyberwar analysts discount the possibility of Chinese cyber weapons being used, the growing consensus is that China is waging a war of espionage across the internet. Cyber espionage is the modern reality in the digtial covert wars.

Surveillance

In times of warfare there is an increased possibility that spies and sympathizers aligned with enemy nations are watching and reporting intelligence to the enemy. Even trivial data can be collated to form a bigger picture – as the old US propaganda posters read, "loose lips sink ships". For this reason suspects possibly indulging in this form of low-level espionage need to be watched at all times. Indeed the formation of the FBI was primarily driven by the awareness of the US authorities that there was a possibility that spies in the First World War were reporting back to Germany. The hunt for the enemy within can only go so far. In a Fascist or Stalinist state everyone becomes the enemy within and the state police and secret services become tools of pure oppression. The problem of the use of the internet for surveillance of citizens – rather than foreigners – is so pervasive that it is dealt with in several chapters later in this book. These modern methods of perpetual surveillance on the internet are so all pervasive that they form a different type of cyberwar: the war against the enemy within is an internal cyberwar being waged by our own governments on their own citizens.

Infiltration

Being able to infiltrate the enemy – or the agents of the enemy – is a vital tool in covert warfare. If you can penetrate the spy-ring of the enemy you can spy on the spies and gain an enormous advantage. If you can control the spy-ring of the enemy, you control all of the information fed to the enemy. In the Second World War, the UK was able to take considerable advantage of the collapse of the Nazi spy-ring by "turning" the spies under threat of possible execution. With little choice but to cooperate, the double agents fed disinformation to the Nazi high command. The use of multiple double agents to report similar findings and sightings helped to validate the incoming information – after all, if all your spies report the same thing, those reports must be the truth. The use of advanced cyber-infiltration techniques allows remote intelligence gathering at a distance, but it is still "human intelligence" gathered by an agent. The use of sock puppets to gather "human intelligence" (HUMINT) with the aim of penetrating Al Qaeda websites is discussed further in Chapter 15, "The Fake Internet".

Sabotage

Low-level sabotage is easy. Just throw a wooden shoe, a "sabot", into some milling machinery and watch it grind to a halt. Sabotage is as simple as sugar in the petrol tank, a missing key, sawdust in the gearbox; the wrong parts packed in a crate or slightly filed firing pins in weapons. Modern digital saboteurs do not need to leave the comfort of their armchair to cause major damage to another country. Cyber sabotage is not fiction, it is a reality. The Stuxnet worm proved that cyber warfare operations in cyberspace could have a drastic effect in the real world – in this case, disrupting the Iranian nuclear program. Even low-level cyberwar waged using simple DDoS tools can have an effect that is far-reaching – as the Russia–Georgia cyber conflict showed. Chapter 13, "Cyber Attack" looks at how the use of cyber weapons can cripple the economy of a country, attack key utilities such as gas, water, electricity and sewage and possibly cause death and destruction on a massive scale.

Psychological Warfare

Psy-ops are an important part of covert warfare. The use of propaganda, counter propaganda and disinformation can be key factors in the psychological manipulation of enemy and allies alike. The internet is a communications medium without equal – we can share rumours, gossip, information and disinformation at the speed of light. But this is not without problems. Hacked Twitter accounts have been used to spread false rumours, which in 2012 caused a US$136.5 billion dip on the Standard & Poor 500 index. The group of cyber-hackivists known as Anonymous are adept at manipulating the media via the internet, and their exfiltration of the HBGary emails was a propaganda coup of major proportions. While waging cyberwar against Libya in 2011, the hacktivist known as The Jester was able to use a little known technique to inject false news stories into *The Tripoli Post* website. We are all at risk. Many of us rely on the internet for information and news, and if the source of the information is possibly contaminated by false news stories, we can no longer form a proper response to the questions and problems that face our society today. The use of sock puppets to influence public opinion on the internet is possibly one of the greatest risks our society faces, but when a nation state actor uses these techniques to change public opinion it can also change foreign policy. The internet is an ideal tool for psychological warfare; the nature of the internet as an instant communications medium makes it the perfect force multiplier for friend and foe alike. The internet itself then becomes a weapon.

Deception

Deception is the key in covert warfare. Without deception the war would not be covert but overt. Sometimes deception is the force multiplier that guarantees success or failure. The Allied deception during the build-up to the D-Day landings in 1944 is a perfect example. Entire brigades of dummy tanks and whole squadrons of dummy aircraft, usually inflatable or made out of wood, were placed in East Anglia to deceive the Nazis into thinking an attack would be in the north of France rather than Normandy. The Nazis were fed false information to convince them that the invasion would be in that region and they moved enough of the military forces into that area to weaken their forces in the true invasion site. In the Cold War, Soviet intelligence agencies were the masters of deception – *maskirovka*, as it was known – as they tried to outfox the US intelligence services with elaborate masquerades. Hiding entire submarine bases under mountains and cutting hidden entrances into the rock face to hide the installations from overhead surveillance satellites was easy if you had an infinite supply of convict labor. These days the Russians use digital *maskirovka* and are capable of successfully hiding their cyber attacks by making it appear that they emanate from another country – China, for example. It has been alleged that Russian cyber-warriors write their malware code in Chinese to make it harder to trace the cyber attacks to Russia. The use of digital *maskirovka* is a fundamental element in the ongoing cyberwars. Who do you blame if you are under cyber attack? Is it a nation state actor or just a bunch of hackers? When servers are subverted and hacked, nobody knows where the attack is really coming from and the problem of global botnets make the problem even more difficult to solve.

If normal covert warfare is a part of ordinary warfare, cyberwar is all these things and more. Cyberwar is global information warfare waged across the internet. The key features of normal covert warfare are the cornerstones of modern digital covert warfare. In the following chapters we will examine the players in this new form of warfare: cyber-hacktivists, cyber-terrorists and cyber-warriors who are backed by nation states. It leads to the inescapable conclusion that cyber weapons are being developed by over 100 different countries and that we are in the middle of a cyber arms race. Cyber attack is now a real possibility that could ruin all of our lives and bring our entire civilization to its knees. The nature of our highly technological society means that we rely on data and code to run our lives, and if the data or code becomes corrupted then the domino effect of cyberwar could destroy society as we know it.

8

WHAT IS CYBERWAR?

What is cyberwar? There is a disagreement among security experts about the nature of cyberwar. Security expert James Andrew Lewis has argued that "no nation has launched a cyber attack or cyberwar against the United States" and that "cyberwar is a risk, a possibility. Espionage and crime in cyberspace are routine occurrences, but they are not acts of war and do not justify the use of military force in response" and that therefore "the cyberwar has not begun." Meanwhile, Richard A. Clarke, a US security expert with close government ties, has defined cyberwar as "actions by a nation state to penetrate another nation's computers or networks for the purpose of causing damage or destruction."[9] To fully understand cyberwar, you need to understand the nature of warfare and military doctrine. Military doctrine is simple: to dominate the battle space whether is on land, at sea, in the air, in space or in cyberspace. When the battle space is in cyberspace, cyberwar is just another tool of information warfare, a possible weapon to deny, destroy and degrade the enemy's capability to wage conventional warfare.

Cyberwar is just an extension of foreign policy by non-conventional means. Information warfare is not new. The techniques being used inside the current cyber-skirmishes have been refined and honed over years but now have far-reaching effects that affect every human being on the planet.

9 *Cyber War: The Next Threat to National Security and What to Do About It*, Richard A. Clarke and Robert K. Knake 2010

"Information Warfare", or "cyberwar" as it has become known, has been a cyber-punk science-fiction staple for many years, but has now become reality. Cyber warfare specialists believe that information warfare is an applied science that can leverage an asymmetrical advantage in the digital battle space. In future warfare the commanders and combatants will use communications across cyberspace to build a picture of the battle space in real time, allowing them to make quick and rapid decisions. This battle space picture will be heavily reliant on maintaining the confidentiality, integrity and access of all the computers and networks that supply that information.

If an enemy has the potential to deny, destroy, and degrade communication networks, to manipulate those networks to intercept communications, to inject disinformation into the information infrastructure and to attack physical infrastructure to gain a tactical or strategic advantage, then they will do so. In this sense, the aims of cyberwar are three fold:

1. To degrade the information infrastructure and communications of the target environment to the point that these channels of communication are unable to function, or are no longer trusted. Direct information infrastructure attacks such as these are designed to degrade the confidence of any potential enemy in their communication abilities, as their channels begin to fail.

2. Cyberwar can also include traditional psychological disinformation techniques, such as PSYOPS, to inject false, misleading and potentially morale-sapping lies and rumours via technical channels of communication.

3. The development of modern cyber weapons allows countries to attack the vital infrastructure of the enemy. Modern cyber weapons not only target cyberspace itself but can reach across cyberspace and target vital infrastructure such as power stations, water pumping stations, refineries, sewage treatment plants and nuclear reactors.

Nation state actors can – and do – plunder the internet with impunity. The use of botnets run by hackers, or the facilities provided by cyber-criminals, makes the new modern digital spies more powerful than a thousand conventional spies. Cyberwar can be waged from the comfort of an office chair, but the impact is as profound as other forms of warfare. The "kinetic option" – the use of bombs, cruise missiles and drones to destroy enemy nation state infrastructure – is obsolete in future cyberwar where the touch of a single key thousands of miles away could cripple entire economies. The last thing to be destroyed will be the internet itself, because without the internet long range cyberwar is impossible – somehow, even in the midst of cyberwar the internet will survive.

Thus the ability of nation states and independent actors to wage cyberwar is a growing problem that affects anybody who uses hi-tech communications devices attached to the internet. If your mobile phone, your Wi-Fi router, your computers are connected to the internet, then cyberwar would inflict massive digital collateral damage. Your printer and other internet-connected devices are a possible digital traitor. If subjected to a cross-site scripting attack that can reach through your firewall, it could attack your printer and force it to print a hundred black pages, endless blank pages or enemy propaganda.

The last thing to be destroyed will be the internet itself, because without the internet long range cyberwar is impossible.

Worse still, the same techniques could be used to wipe out the flash **BIOS** and reduce your expensive printer to nothing more than a piece of electronic junk. Using internet updates to replace a firmware BIOS is a good idea, but a sustained cyberwar attack against vulnerable firmware could reduce large portions of the internet to inert pieces of plastic and useless silicon circuitry. The use of modern techniques to upgrade the BIOS of your computer from the internet is a hidden threat to every user.

However it does seem likely that any form of cyberwar between conflicting nations states would be backed up with conventional military options. If a full-blown cyberwar breaks out on a global scale, it will almost certainly be a part of the Third World War. Meanwhile, there are a number of minor digital skirmishes and brush-fire cyberwars raging across cyberspace as cyber-hacktivists and terrorists continue their attacks.

But do the large power blocs such as the USA, Russia and China consider that the Third World War will really be fought in the cyberspace?

The answer is yes. From the evidence presented below, it becomes obvious that the domination of cyberspace during times of international tension is becoming increasingly important and that some countries are more prepared than others. Until recently, theorists who spoke about the coming cyberwar and the possibilities of cyber warfare were ignored as threat-mongers and hawks. Now that has changed and all branches of the military are rushing to add cyber warfare capabilities to their armed forces. But what makes cyberwar so attractive to nation states, and what would be gained by pursuing overt or covert information warfare?

Thus in a very real sense we are already inside a low-level cyberwar. This type of cyberwar is so commonplace that we have become used to it. We live with the threat on a daily basis and use firewalls and anti-virus software to combat it. The growth of cybercrime over the last few years has provided dark-side programmers the ability to construct ever more complex malware – worms have replaced viruses and RATs have become commonplace. The use of large numbers of compromised zombie computers arranged into botnets allows massive distributed denial of service attacks on a scale that was previously impossible. When thousands or even hundreds of thousands of computers attack an internet server at the same time, it will be brought to its knees in no time at all.

Future cyber-warriors will use many of the same techniques as the black hat hackers and cyber-criminals. Cyber-warriors will use sophisticated techniques using zero day vulnerabilities to inject malware such as rootkits, keyloggers and RATs with the sole purpose of cyber warfare on a global scale. They will also use social engineering attacks, phishing, spear phishing and any other attacks necessary for gaining access to specific targets. By targeting personal information such as usernames and passwords, cyber-warriors can gain entry into the "circle of trust" of the target and exploit this to gain even more information, which in turn can be used for further social engineering and possible disinformation attacks. By targeting the information used for financial transactions across the web – credentials for online banking, credit card information and passwords for eBay and PayPal accounts – cyber-warriors can cause chaos by theft or maybe just allow the covert and illegal transfer of funds to finance black operations in the real world. The use of these types of techniques by militant cyber-terrorists is documented in Chapter 13 (see page 131).

Because cyberwar will use well known methods of hacking that are known and used by hackers and cyber-criminals, it will be hard to know when cyberwar has broken out. The use of black hat techniques to subvert and compromise computers for profit are well known. If a series of cyber attacks motivated by national policy are launched across the web using similar tactics, then it will be hard to make proper attribution for those attacks. Nobody will know where those attacks are coming from. We have already grown used to the antics of cyber-activists and hacktivists who use this low level of cyberwar for attacking those corporations and organizations to which they are ideologically or politically opposed. The constant background noise of modern cyber threat allows the cyber-warrior to hide amongst the cyber-hacktivists and criminals, allowing for effective covert digital warfare. When cyberwar breaks out, it could take a long time to realize it.

This extends to espionage. Reporters and industrial spies often use hacking skills – or hackers themselves – to gather information about individuals or corporations. The recent UK scandals about the use of phone-hacking by newspapers and industrial spies is a case in point. Information about hacking voice mailboxes and answer phones has been a staple of hacker text files since the earliest hacker bulletin board systems and now these techniques have trickled down from the hacker world into the hands of people who don't just hack for fun. The wider use of known hacking techniques by nation state actors is important. When it was revealed that Operation Aurora had possibly exfiltrated the Google source code it was widely assumed that China was responsible. Even though all the circumstantial evidence points to Chinese involvement the repeated denials by the Chinese government and the lack of a "smoking gun" means that nobody can be 100% certain of Chinese involvement. Anybody could have wanted the Google source code for any reason. Kevin Mitnick was alleged to have downloaded the source code for the VAX VMS operating system because he was motivated by curiosity. He was not an industrial spy or cyber-warrior from a foreign country; he was a hobbyist hacker with a thirst for knowledge. Hackers are notoriously curious about the workings of computers and stealing the source code for Google would allow a glimpse into the inner workings of the most famous search engine on the planet.

Cyberwar turns the hacker ethic upside down. For a long time, many hackers adhered to a code of behavior that included not tampering with data and not damaging computers in any way. Any future cyberwar will rely on destroying both data and computers.

We have arrived at a point where we can differentiate between the normal low-level cyber warfare conducted on a daily basis by hackers and cyber-criminals and the type of high level cyberwar that will be waged in the future.

1. The use of cyberwar is sanctioned by a nation state. Resources are allocated to cyber-warriors for the development and testing of cyber weapons. A program of training is undertaken to form a "digital cadre" who can learn and pass their skills to the next generation. New units are formed which are incorporated into the military hierarchy, such as the recent formation of the United States Cyber Command (USCYBERCOM).

2. The use of cyberwar is seen as an extension of normal warfare. Within the military doctrine of the USA, the battle space has traditionally been seen as the four domains of land, sea, air and space. With the formation of the United States Cyber Command, it can now be seen that cyberspace has been accepted as the "fifth domain". Now military policy accepts that it has to achieve full spectrum dominance over all five domains, it is inevitable that the militarization of cyberspace will begin.

3. Just as traditional warfare is dictated by foreign policy, so is cyberwar. Once it is accepted that cyberwar exists, then a country can begin to debate important questions. What is an act of cyberwar? How can the perpetrator of such acts be traced? What is the correct diplomatic or military response to an act of cyberwar? These questions are now starting to be debated openly by governments everywhere and could lead to a code of conduct for cyber conflict similar to the Geneva convention.

4. The use of cyberwar is integrated into traditional covert warfare, allowing for "black operations" to be performed across cyberspace. The use of digital espionage using the internet is highly effective and the evidence suggests that a number of countries, including Russia, China and Israel, have integrated cyberspace into their normal espionage operations. Even if the USA created and unleashed the Stuxnet worm, it still required old-fashioned espionage both to

gather information about the Iranian nuclear program and possibly to insert the worm into the Iranian computer systems.

5. Research and development of true cyber weapons has begun, making a cyber arms race inevitable and cyberwar more likely. These cyber weapons will begin as versions of hacking tools used by cyber-criminals and become more sophisticated over time. Already the US government has started to purchase zero day vulnerabilities from the criminal hackers – these exploits will be packaged into new cyber weapons that guarantee a successful attack. The Stuxnet worm used four different zero day vulnerabilities to penetrate the Iranian system, but future cyber weapons will use more.

6. Just as conventional warfare readiness exercises are routinely used to train soldiers, cyber exercises that simulate cyber conflict will be used. This has already begun in the USA: "Cyber Storm" in 2006 simulated a cyber conflict that attacked critical infrastructure and "Cyber Shockwave" in 2010 included a scenario where 60 million smart phones were disabled by malware. The USA is not alone in preparing for cyberwar. In 2013, China conducted its first cyber-readiness exercise designed to test new types of combat forces that included digital technology.

Thus cyberwar is a low intensity form of warfare that leverages the maximum benefit from the least cost. It is an ideal force multiplier that supports and enhances military operations across the entire battle space. For smaller countries, cyberwar is ideal for force projection in an **asymmetrical conflict**. It is a form of modern "cold warfare" where opposing nation states seek economic or political advantage but wish to avoid open conflict. Cyberwar is relatively easy to perform and will almost certainly realize benefits over and above the small cost of investment.

So, why would any nation state choose cyberwar over other forms of conflict? The relative ease. It was originally estimated that in order to mount and succeed in an attempted "Cyber Pearl Harbor", an enemy nation with cyber warfare would need $200 million dollars and five years of preparation, but the latest developments in cyber weaponry now put this in doubt. There a number of reasons why a country might find cyberwar an attractive proposition.

Low cost

For countries that are banned from importing hi-tech weaponry, or who are too poor to buy weapons, cyberwar is a low cost alternative. Once internet infrastructure is in place, it is possible to train a cadre of cyberwar specialists and begin weapons development. In some countries that could be classed as gangster states, the levels of corruption mean that governments can buy entire networking infrastructures to use as a platform for future cyber attacks. Meanwhile those infrastructures are used for **bullet proof hosting**, botnet command and control and phishing sites.

Low Risk

The use of cyberwar is a low risk activity for the attacking country. If conducted correctly, it will be impossible to determine which country is doing the attacking and difficult to form a response. Furthermore, modern state of the art rootkits can mean that malware can be undetected for months if not years. By the time the malware is discovered, it will be impossible to determine the culprit. Many countries with low GDP use pirated copies of the Microsoft operating system and fail to update their computers with security patches. It would be possible to infect the computers of an entire country without being detected until the malware was triggered – and by then attempts to counter it would be too late.

Low Visibility

The nature of covert digital warfare means that it is conducted under the radar. This is especially true when the attack is distributed across many small groups who attack a target independently. Groups that appear to be cyber-hacktivists or cyber-terrorists could actually be state-sponsored. Countries engaged in cyberwar are prepared to turn a blind eye to groups which are truly independent, provided they do not attack economic or internet resources in their own country. There is evidence that both Russia and China permit these types of activities in their countries.

Proxy Actors

Nation states engaged in cyberwar can use proxies to perform attacks. Why bother building a botnet to attack internet infrastructure when it is easy and cheap to hire one? Why recruit a cadre of programmers to design and build malware when the digital underground is full of black hat programmers for hire? To go one step further, there is no reason why a determined cyber enemy could not buy the services of an entire country with economic or political inducements. In the cold war this type of proxy agent used by both the USA and the USSR was commonplace, and it is likely that cyberwar will also use countries to fight proxy digital wars.

Plausible Deniability

The nature of the internet means that the use of digital *maskirovka* to maintain plausible deniability during a cyberwar is a certainty. Because the tools and techniques used by cyber-warriors are virtually identical to those used by cyber-hacktivists, cyber-terrorists and cyber-criminals, any one of these groups can be used as a "patsy"and blamed for the attacks. Even if cyberwar attacks are pinpointed from a certain country, there is always some doubt whether the perpetrators were from that country. Plausible deniability and the chance of avoiding politically embarrassing blowback is the key to waging modern cyber war.

The mounting evidence that Russia and China have been engaged in cyber espionage can be countered by traditional propaganda and press releases along traditional lines. If you repeat the "big lie" long enough, then people will believe it. This is pure Cold War thinking updated for the modern world. For example:

> *"Just because this spate of attacks originated from Russia/China does not mean that our country is responsible."*

> *"Accusing Russia/China of these alleged penetrations is further evidence of Cold War thinking on the part of the US government and a blatant attempt to foster a digital arms race."*

"Those damned cyber-criminals! We are trying to stamp them out, but you understand this is a global problem and we are doing the best we can."

"These attacks appeared to have been launched from our country, but further analysis shows that the alleged intrusions were from somewhere outside of our domain."

We can conclude that in times of world crisis there will be a corresponding increase in cyberwar attacks. The low cost, low risk and low visibility of cyberwar has led to an estimated 100 countries preparing or developing cyber warfare capabilities. Cyberwar is a reality now, despite the carping of some pundits, and it will be more prevalent in the future. The rapid integration of cyberwar into the US military hierarchy supports the idea that we are in a cyber arms race. Things are going to get a lot worse before they get better – if they get better at all. Now the stage is set. It is time to introduce the main actors in the current cyberwars: hacktivists, terrorists and the military.

9

CYBER-HACKTIVISM

There is a fine line between cyber-activism and cyber-hacktivism and that line begins right outside of a prison cell. Cyber-activists use the internet in an effective way to promote their message through websites and social networking sites, but they do not break the law. Cyber-activists are using the internet as a medium of communication, like the use of broadsheets newspapers in the Victorian era, to influence public opinion. Although anyone can make and distribute a website, it might be illegal to do so for certain opposition groups who are perceived to be a threat to the state.

Cyber-activists are an important part of the entire democratic process on which our civilization depends. Their use of cyber-technology and social networks facilitates the ongoing debate about how we allow our society to function and benefits everyone. We should all have access to information and debate about what that information means, and having a multitude of open source alternative websites can only be a good thing for our modern digital society.

Like corporations, modern cyber-activism uses the internet as the "fifth domain" of publicity. The use of digital media and crowd-sourcing, as well as the use of social networking sites such as Facebook and YouTube. to spread their message goes far beyond mimeographed handouts at a demonstration. Skilled and sophisticated users of the internet can spread memes across the web at the speed of light and it is their right to do so. Theoretically anyone can build a website, a weblog or a forum in cyberspace and it is right that they do so. Free speech and open debate are the cornerstones of a modern democracy and the internet is a great force multiplier that facilitates small groups.

But there is a great difference between cyber-activists and the cyber hacktivists – hacktivists break the law. Hacktivists break into computers and embarrass multinational companies and media companies. In 2011 the hacktivist group "LulzSec" attacked a public CIA website with a massive "distributed denial of service" attack. For that reason, some of them were hunted down, caught and prosecuted. The recent FBI arrests of members of Anonymous and Lulzsec might have damaged hacktivism, but it is not dead. The motto of Anonymous haunts me: "We Are Legion, We Are Many", and somewhere out on the internet Anonymous are almost certainly planning their next outrage.

Anonymous

Who are Anonymous? Once, nobody knew the identity of this shadowy collective of hacktivists, but recent events have unmasked some of the people who hide behind the mask of Anonymous. Some people call them "digital terrorists" while others call them "hackers on steroids"; it depends on your viewpoint. It is generally accepted that the amorphous collective hive-mind behind Anonymous evolved out of a sub-culture of image based internet bulletin boards such as "4chan", which not only allowed anonymous posting but also encouraged it.

Anonymous grew out of the the forum "4chan" sometime around 2004. They soon discovered a shared collective love of pulling internet pranks on unsuspecting users. By 2006 they were organising digital flash mobs to invade websites such as "Habbo" or "Second Life" and enjoying the chaos that they caused. What are the motivations of Anonymous? Let them speak in their own words: "We are the face of chaos and the harbingers of judgment. We'll laugh in the face of tragedy. We'll mock those who are in pain. We ruin the lives of other people simply because we can. A man takes out his aggression on the cat. We laugh. Hundreds die in a plane crash. We laugh. The nation mourns over school shootings, we laugh. We're the embodiment of humanity with no remorse, no caring, no love, or no sense of morality. We only have the desire for more and more. And now quite simply you have got our attention." The Anonymous collective are a perfect example of online crowd-sourcing.

They are a "digital fractal society": every time you try and find one member, there are more. With no leaders, there is no leadership. The use of a cell structure and cut-offs are perfect examples of Cold War tradecraft in action. In the new modern digital age of cyber attack, Anonymous are a force multiplier for hacktivists everywhere. Their model of distributed cyber attacks will be noted by our enemies, and our allies, alike. Anonymous are not a group. Anonymous are an idea – a digital virus that affects everybody. In the new digital cyberwars, ideas are more important than computer code or data. The new digital wars will be fought with ideas, using the internet as the primary weapon.

Anonymous propagated itself across the internet at the speed of light, occupying large portions of the web using websites, IRCs, social networking sites such as Facebook or Twitter and YouTube. The use of multiple vectors of internet communication allowed a decentralized but somehow coordinated wave of attacks across the internet. Anonymous were the first of the hacktivist groups to go beyond the limits of the law. Anonymous not only crossed the line – they tried to erase the line altogether.

Project Chanology, 2008

One of the earliest attempts to use online coordinated crowd-sourced attacks using the internet were the early attacks on the Church of Scientology, which tried to remove alleged copyrighted material from the internet. Of course, the nature of data being what it is, as fast as once site was removed, ten others would spring up to replace them. It should be noted that many old-school hackers still bear antipathy to the Church of Scientology for their takedown of the anon.penet.fi remailer, which allowed truly anonymous communication with both USENET and other email addresses. As Anonymous say, "We Never Forget. We Never Forgive", so the attacks could have been expected by any long-time internet user with an interest in computer security and hacking.

The Anonymous attacks on the Church of Scientology were crude at the time – prank phone calls, black blank faxes and various online attacks were the order of the day. Interestingly, at this time, the Guy Fawkes mask from V for Vendetta made its first appearance at physical protests. More than anything, this image defines Anonymous in the collective psyche of the public and has been copied across the world to epitomize an image of defiance that transcends anything that Anonymous have ever accomplished in cyberspace.

Operation Payback, 2010

What would the modern world be like without WikiLeaks? The truth is that Wikileaks was started by the ex-hacker Mendax as a source of leaked documents from whistle-blowers to reveal any secret. Fine in principle, but after the release of the video entitled Collateral Murder, followed by the release of many secret US diplomatic cables, the knives were out for Wikileaks. After the publication of hundreds of confidential and secret documents, it is alleged that the US government placed pressure on the providers of online payment services such as PayPal, MasterCard and Visa to curtail the inflow of donations to Wikileaks by cutting off their payment services.

Then Anonymous stepped in and began an orchestrated Distributed Denial of Service (DDoS) attack on the websites of the companies allegedly involved in the embargo. Whether the campaign had any long-term effect is debatable. Some sources deny that there was no disruption to the Visa and MasterCard websites, but Anonymous claimed success. This time the world sat up and paid attention. The FBI and local police issued warrants for over 40 members who were alleged to be part of Anonymous, mostly low level foot soldiers who had been using the Low Orbit Ion Cannon (LOIC) denial of service tool against the target websites. There was, as we shall see later, a reason for this: a lone wolf patriot hacktivist had hacked the binary code and made it much less anonymous, leading to a large number of arrests of Anonymous cannon fodder.

HBGary Federal, 2011

The scene was now set for the most audacious hacking attack by Anonymous since their formation in 2004. When the FBI and certain computer security companies alleged they had tracked down the leaders of Anonymous, the collective counterattacked in a way that sent shivers down the spine of every member of the computer security industry.

Anonymous hacked into the corporate servers of HBGary Federal and stole hundreds of confidential and semi-confidential documents, including an entire archive of private emails. When they released the documents on the internet, it was discovered that certain computer security companies are actively developing rootkit and malware software using zero day vulnerabilities for corporate use. The inherent dangers in writing malware for corporate usage are huge. Once corporate malware is released on the internet, cyber-criminals will soon copy it, reverse engineer it and rewrite it for their own use. The impact in the average internet user would be massive, as the malware development process will now include information gleaned from professionally written malware. This could lead to an explosion of malware that is more sophisticated and more dangerous than ever before. Although the revelations from the stolen email archives will come as no surprise to any long-term observer of the hacking scene, this information led the US Congress to call for an investigation into corporate malware. The scandal caused by the Anomymous attack was sufficient that the CEO of HBGary Federal Aaron Barr resigned that same year while corporate partners such as Palantir and Berico Technologies "scrambled to distance themselves" from the public relations disaster.[10]

LulzSec

By 2011, a group of hackers – who may or may not have been aligned with Anonymous – became LulzSec. The name derives from the internet acronym LOL (for Laugh Out Loud) but has been subverted to a much darker purpose. Unlike a LOL, a LUL is an evil Laugh Out Loud. A LUL is the laughter of someone who thrives on digital *schadenfreude* – the sort of evil hacker who takes delight invading and destroying popular internet virtual spaces, just for the LULZ. When you hack for the LULZ, the major aim is subverting, discomforting and embarrassing your target – there is no political purpose. As LulzSec said themselves, "we do things just because we find it entertaining... you find it funny to watch havoc unfold, and we

10 Andy Greenberg, "HBGary Federal's Aaron Barr Resigns After Anonymous Hack Scandal" Forbes, 2011

find it funny to cause it. We release personal data so that equally evil people can entertain us with what they do with it."

LulzSec were an elite band of digital criminals… but this was to be their downfall. At one point their exploits made them the number one hacktivist group in the world. When LulzSec first launched onto the hacking scene in 2011, they used the mocking slogan "Laughing at your security since 2011". They might have been right because they proceeded to hack their way across the internet, claiming responsibility for several high-profile hacks, including Sony Pictures, the UK's National Health Service (NHS) and even the CIA. Stealing data and publishing it online was their favourite pastime. During the time that LulzSec were engaged in their hacking spree, they published nearly a million user credentials and email addresses on the web for anyone to use.

When you hack for the LULZ the major aim is subverting, discomforting and embarrassing your target – there is no political purpose.

Unlike Anonymous, LulzSec had a highly centralized organization – an estimated seven core members with very few affiliated hackers. This highly centralized organizational structure was to be the downfall of LulzSec. When the FBI identified the alleged leader of LulzSec, known by the online handle Sabu, as Hector Xavier Monsegur, the reign of digital terror caused by LulzSec was close to coming to an end. In a masterpiece of digital **counter intelligence** (COINTELPRO), the FBI "turned" Sabu and offered him a deal. Now that the leader of LulzSec was a federal informer, LulzSec would be taken down from within.

Within weeks coordinated raids in the USA and the UK led to the arrest of the core members of the group. In 2013, four hackers from the UK, known online as Kayla, Topiary, Tflow and Viral were sentenced to prison terms ranging from a suspended sentence of 20 months up to 32 months. Two other members of LulzSec, known as Pwnsauce and Palladium, were luckier because the Irish authorities refused to press charges. The US hacker known as Anarchaos, who had possible links to the Anonymous collective, faces up to 10 years in prison for his role in the hacking of computer security company "Stratfor". Meanwhile, Sabu, the alleged mastermind behind the LuzSec cyber gang, is awaiting sentencing, but it is highly likely that he will evade a whole slew of unrelated charges. Even though Sabu could face an estimated 124 years in prison for the 12 charges he has confessed to, it still seems likely that his continuing cooperation with the FBI will guarantee a light sentence or even participation in the witness protection program.

The success of the FBI operation was a classic informant sting. Without the help of Sabu, it would have been much harder to identify the other members of the hacktivist group. By infiltrating LulzSec at the highest level, the FBI was able to take down the group in a very short time. But did they have help? There are some who claimed the FBI was helped by the mysterious hacker known only as The Jester.

The Jester

Who is The Jester? (AKA "th3j35t3r") Nobody knows – and although many have tried to unmask this digital vigilante, nobody has succeeded to date. What is known about The Jester is very interesting indeed. The Jester is a patriot hacker, a hacktivist who uses his skills to attack the perceived enemies of the USA. This is not surprising. Evidence suggests that The Jester was at one time associated with the military and might possibly have served in Afghanistan.[11]

This also explains the main targets of The Jester – internet websites that offer a platform for terrorists to spread propaganda, recruit new members and offer lethal online guides about how to construct Improvised Explosive Devices (IEDs) and suicide vests. In 2010, The Jester began his campaign against pro-Jihad websites using DDoS attacks. In the next two years over 75 pro-Jihad websites were attacked – but the Jester did not stop there.

It now seems likely that The Jester was one of the many "patriot hackers" who attacked the WikiLeaks website with a DDoS attack, taking it temporarily offline. Attacks like these soon forced WikiLeaks to employ new servers that were more resistant to attack – but at a price. When

11 O'Connor, SANS Institute, *The Jester Dynamic: A Lesson in Asymmetric Unmanaged Cyber Warfare* 2011

Anonymous announced Operation Payback (see page 77) in support of WikiLeaks, The Jester intervened.

In a masterpiece of hacking, The Jester reverse-engineered the Anonymous approved DDoS tool LOIC and published his own version of the malware. This hacked version of the malware had all the anonymizing functionally removed, effectively exposing the IP address of any Anonymous supporters using the tool against the PayPal, MasterCard and Visa websites. This deception worked well enough that over the next few months, 24 Anonymous members were arrested for their part in the denial of service attacks.

The Jester refused to remain idle. After exposing members of Anonymous, he turned his attention to LulzSec. Within a week, Viral was under arrest and very soon The Jester correctly identified Sabu, the leader of LulzSec, as Hector Xavier Monsegur. Very soon the FBI had arrested and turned Sabu. All evidence suggests that it was The Jester who unmasked LulzSec – and passed the information to the FBI.

The most surprising thing about The Jester is his skill in the use of social media to promote and disseminate his ideas. He has a regular weblog where he can be contacted and his Twitter account has around 28,000 followers. He is no stranger to publicity and regularly tweets when he has attacked a target, making him one of the highest profile hackers on the internet today. Despite all of this he has remained anonymous: even though fifteen people have been alleged to be The Jester, his true identity still remains unknown at the time of writing.

Conclusion

If all hacktivists are breaking the law, how do they differ? We have seen that there is a huge difference between cyber-activism and cyber-hacktivism. Although at times they may appear similar, responsible pressure groups rarely cross the line into cyber-criminal activity. Hacktivists are different. Hacktivists use illegal hacking techniques for a variety of purposes and this chapter has examined the three most common motivations.

It is quite obvious that Anonymous are breaking the law but their intention is subversion, embarrassment, and the art of data-theft as schadenfreude. It is the art of data-theft as art itself. In this way they seem to me to have updated the French Situationist International (SI) movement (1957–1972) for cyberspace in the twenty-first century.

Anonymous are using "digital *détournement*" to overthrow our preconceived notions of cyberspace. Their repeated use of data-theft and subsequent release of that data – removing all worth from the data itself, challenges our ideas about internet security and data privacy. Private data makes money, but as we have seen in the case of Anonymous, private data in the public view makes for a scandal.

> **Anonymous's repeated use of data-theft and subsequent release of that data – removing all worth from the data itself, challenges our ideas about internet security and data privacy.**

Then there is the case of LulzSec, a group of digital scofflaws who openly mocked authority by stealing and publishing huge amounts of confidential data. If Anonymous could be likened to the Situationist International (SI) movement, then LulzSec are more like the Merry Pranksters of the sixties or maybe even the Youth International Party ("Yippies"). The Yippies did not just use the conventional protest methods of the time. They made the art of détournement popular in the USA by trying to levitate the Pentagon building and running a pig for presidential office. More importantly for the hacking community, they started the seminal phreaking magazine TAP, which enabled a whole generation of young hackers to play with the phone system for fun. LulzSec are the latest in a long line of hackers who like to hack… just for the "LULZ".

Finally, the Joker in the pack: The Jester. Lone-wolf hactivism is rare – but guarantees a high-degree of security against being caught. The questions surrounding the identity of The Jester are important, because we cannot know for sure who is protecting him. It is interesting to note that no patriot hackers who attacked WikiLeaks with DDoS attacks were ever identified and prosecuted – but the LulzSec hackers were identified and prosecuted in a short space of time. Is the US government itself protecting The Jester? Has the US government finally wised up to the techniques used by the Chinese and Russian cyber-warriors? A digital vigilante such as The Jester is a useful weapon in the covert digital wars of today, allowing full plausible deniability and expendability – as long as he attacks enemies of the USA.

We are entering a new age of covert digital warfare, where hacktivist groups appear to be using conventional hacker tools to break into websites, computers and organizations on a daily basis. Are these hacktivists really who they seem? Or are they sock puppets in the ongoing cyberwars?

How much of the ongoing cyberwars are nothing more than digital *maskirovka*? From all the current evidence, Anonymous and LulzSec have been heavily penetrated by law enforcement efforts. This leads to the possibility of external takeover and control of alleged hacktivist groups – who are then nothing more than useful tools for nation state actors. It is akin to the Cold War funding of various terrorist and political organizations by the USSR and the USA: you never know which front group is working for which faction. Some people have even suggested that Julian Assange, one of the co-founders of WikiLeaks, is in reality a CIA asset.

Digital espionage is the grandchild of conventional espionage, but the use of the internet allows for interesting possibilities in the eternal game of cat-and-mouse of double and triple agents – a cyber-world of digital shadows where nobody can be trusted. The use of digital *maskirovka* allows governments and corporations to build a fake internet, where online reality is nothing more than phony websites, propaganda and sock puppets. This is a digital shadow-world where nothing is what it seems. We shall return to this theme in Chapter 15, "The Fake Internet" (page 149).

10

CYBER-TERRORISM

Defining cyber-terrorism is as difficult as defining cyberspace itself. What is the difference between cyber-terrorism and cyber-hacktivism? The actions of Anonymous have led to some journalists calling the Anonymous collective "domestic terrorists". Are they really cyber-terrorists? To get to the heart of the problem we need to define terrorism itself – which is no easy task either.

As the saying goes, "one man's terrorist is another man's freedom fighter". Are members of the IRA (Irish Republican Army) "terrorists" or "freedom fighters"? Are members of ETA (Euskadi Ta Askatasuna) "terrorists" or "freedom fighters"? There is a fine line to be drawn in the sand and it depends on what side you are on.

In general, terrorism can be described as the use of violence, or the threat of violence to cause fear, panic and demoralization of a community in pursuit of a political or religious goal. Terrorists are usually very good at manipulating the media for maximum impact – each terrorist action is designed to cause shock and awe.

Defining cyber-terrorism as a form of conventional terrorist behavior allows us to think about the difference between hacktivists and cyber-terrorists. The tools and techniques remain the same but the motivation makes all the difference to the threat. The major difference is that for terrorists violence is always an option. Hacktivist groups like Anonymous are unlikely to start using suicide bombers to make their point – for them, the battle space is the internet itself and their weapons are computers.

The historic definition of terrorism grew in popularity after the attacks in the 1960's and 1970's. For the hard left and hard right (who were more inclined to violence) terrorism was trendy. They often openly supported actions of terrorists even when the motivation was dubious at best. Civil disobedience was hip and pinning a picture of a Molotov cocktail on your wall was an open statement of dissent. Even if you never made a Molotov cocktail, you could dream. For many people then, the overthrow of the state was only a matter of time. Some became disillusioned with the political process and decided that violence – killing, shooting, bombing, and stealing – was the only way to further their personal and political goals.

But what were the motivations of the terrorists? How were they different between the terrorists of today? Back then, the threat landscape was different, and it has sinc evolved. Now the biggest threat is Islamic militant terrorism but all types of terrorist groups can use the internet in the same way.

Right-wing Terrorism

Right-wing terrorism wants to replace the state with a dictatorship of the mind. Anyone who disagrees with them will be exterminated. In the mindset of many right-wing terrorists, the USA is an occupied territory and under the power of the Zionist Occupational Government (ZOG), which must be overthrown at all costs.

The Oklahoma bombing in 1995 by nationalist and patriotic groups alerted the US government to the possibility of right-wing groups that wanted to overthrow the government and constitution. Because of this, the militia and right wing groups are profiled and watched just as much as members of Al-Qaeda. There are enough dissidents within the USA to cause major problems for the government. The threat of the enemy within is enough excuse to build a perpetual surveillance society where police states can build a digital **panopticon** where everyone is watched all of the time.

Left-wing Terrorism

Left-wing terrorism seeks to replace the current "bourgeois capitalist hegemony" with a society that is arranged according to the ideology of the Marxist–Leninism philosophy, and a dash of Maoism. In the late

Sixties and early Seventies terrorists such as the Red Army Faction (RAF) and the Baader Meinhof gang were infamous across central Europe. In England, the anarchistic Angry Brigade committed 25 bombings, while in the USA the Weather Underground Organization or Weathermen – named after a line in a Bob Dylan song – committed various robberies and bombings.

Many left-wing terrorist groups were infiltrated by undercover agents in COINTELPRO operations specifically designed to destabilize and sow mistrust against counter-culture groups that were deemed to be in opposition to the state. Other terrorist groups were wiped out in clashes with the police and others were imprisoned. The phenomenon of far-left terrorism virtually died out after the fall of the Berlin Wall in 1989. The collapse of communism left a political void in which revolution seemed much less likely and acts of left-wing terrorism dropped off significantly – but modern groups such as the anti-globalization protesters are adept at using the internet to plan civil disobedience on a grand scale.

Nationalist Terrorism

The motivation of the nationalist terrorists makes them much more like true insurgents than other types of terrorists. They normally see themselves as freedom fighters whose sole goal in performing acts of terrorism is either to overthrow the current government or to liberate their country from what they perceive as colonialist oppression by a larger nation. Both the Irish Republican Army (IRA) and the Basque terrorist group Euskadi Ta Askatasuna (ETA) are typical groups of this type. Although frequent ceasefires are arranged between the ruling governments and these types of terrorist groups, and although some groups become inactive for long periods of time, the threat of nationalist terrorism can return at any time if the nationalist groups feel aggrieved.

Palestinian Terrorism

It could be argued that terrorism by Palestinian refugees against global targets to draw attention to their continuing armed struggle is a form of nationalis terrorism. Certainly the Palestinians regard the Israeli government as an occupying force in their homeland, but there are important differences between the various Palestinian terrorist groups such as Fatah, Hezbollah and other nationalist terror groups. Indeed, Hamas is a government in its own right even though described by the USA as a terrorist organization.

The major difference is that the spate of attacks in the Seventies and Eighties – the Munich massacre, the Lod airport attack and the hijacking of the Achille Lauro – allowed the formation of an experienced cadre of terrorists from an Islamic background. This cadre have been central in teaching the new generation of terrorists who form the amorphous group that is called Al Qaeda – the first truly transnational terrorist organization, which draws members from multiple countries – all of which have many similar beliefs in common.

The growth of the web, social media and instant communication facilitates terrorism just as it facilitates modern life.

Early terrorist groups were highly adept in the use of the media as manifesto. Every hijack became a television show, every proclamation became news and every death sent a shock through the world.

This media exposure allowed the terrorists to spread their message across the globe. If early terrorists were highly effective in spreading their infectious memes across the planet, then modern terrorists are even better. The growth of the web, social media and instant communication facilitates terrorism just as it facilitates modern life.

In the seeds of the terrorism of the past, we can see the forest of the future. While other terrorist groups have either been crushed or have almost given up, the groups behind the pro-Palestinian terrorist protests have evolved. There are no significant right-wing or left-wing terrorist groups left on the planet to plan attacks with the skill of the militant Jihadi terrorist organizations. With the US announcement of the War on Terror, law enforcement efforts have been focused on homegrown pro-militant Jihadi terrorist cells from all over the world. This new enemy within has made the internet their home.

If the early terrorists were a cadre that trained the terrorists of the future, the modern terrorist cadres are using the internet as a weapon to train the next cadre of terrorists. This new digital cadre of pro-militant Jihadis are using the internet to spread their message of hate. The militant Jihadis may hate the USA as the "Great Satan", but they were quick to spot the potential of the internet (first developed in the USA) as a force multiplier in their struggle against their enemy. If you can spread your propaganda quickly and cheaply across the internet, this is more effective than a thousand printing presses and even better than owning a TV station.

Militant Jihadi Terrorism

Today the USA perceives radical Islamic Jihadi terrorism as the number one threat. This is not surprising after the attacks in Nairobi and Tanzania in 1998, in the Yemen in 2000, and on American soil on September 11, 2001, which destroyed the twin towers of the World Trade Center – live and direct – shocking everyone around the world. Al Qaeda had arrived, and everybody now knew who Osama Bin Laden was.

The open nature of the internet is the friend of a militant Jihadi terrorist. It is a place to share information, plan attacks and ferment hatred. If the number one terrorist threat on the planet today is Al-Qaeda and affiliates, then the number two threat is the internet itself. Jihadi terrorists have made the internet their home and they use it in a variety of ways.

- Distribution of hate material: Videos excoriating the "great Satan" or Israel, fatwas and general propaganda that incites an atmosphere of hatred against the enemy.
- Distribution of Jihadi videos: Homemade videos of Jihadi attacks on international troops in both Iraq and Afghanistan are copied around the globe. These are a powerful morale booster for other terrorists considering attacks.
- Distribution of training material: Operations manuals, weapon manuals and bomb-making manuals are shared on Jihadi websites. Videos covering the manufacture of improvised explosive devices (IEDs) are commonplace.

- Distribution of counterintelligence material: Information about law enforcement techniques and intelligence operations. Manuals on good old-fashioned cold war tradecraft so beloved of spy authors.
- Online Forums: Online forums allow Jihadi terrorists and fellow travellers a means of communication. The use of Arabic as the forum language makes it hard for many western analysts to penetrate. There are groups of counter terrorist experts who seek out and monitor online forums of this kind, but these can be hard to find. Online forums provide a platform for recruitment, information sharing and the planning of attacks.
- Hacktivism: Supporters of militant Jihad regularly attack websites in the USA and Israel, especially at times of heightened tension or actual conflict. Web defacement and denial of service are common, but pro-Jihadi hacktivists also break into servers in order to store videos and training material.
- Cybercrime: This activity is motivated not by profit (as with most cybercrime) but by the terrorist beliefs of the militants. The case of "Irhabi007" below illustrates this trend. Cyber-terrorists use the same techniques as cyber-criminals and hacktivists, but their only motivation is to promote militant Jihadi terrorism.

When Younes Tsouli, a 23 year-old IT student, and son of a Moroccan diplomat, was exposed to Jihadi videos, he became involved in cyber-terrorism. Tsouli and his two friends, Tariq Al-Daour, a 21-year-old student of biochemistry and Waseem Mughal, a 24-year-old law student, would soon become the most successful cyber-terrorist cell ever known. When Tsouli started hanging out on cyber-terrorist forums, he adopted the hacker handle Irhabi007, a portmanteau name derived from the Arabic for "terrorist" and the codename of James Bond.

But Irhabi007 wanted to distribute more than ordinary propaganda videos. Apart from distributing normal terrorist material such as manuals for electronic Jihad, extremist videos, training material and other propaganda, Irhabi007 had more hardcore material. These videos showed military attacks on US forces, suicide bombings, hostage beheading and training videos on how to construct IEDs and suicide vests. Irhabi007 became an asset for the cyber-terrorist propaganda machine and by 2004 had been noticed by Al Qaeda itself, who were having problems distributing their propaganda videos.

Irhabi007 took his cyber-terrorism seriously and used hacking techniques to compromise a large number of servers, which became hosts for Al Qaeda propaganda. As Irhabi007 improved his hacking skills he became more important, and by 2005, Irhabi007 was the administrator of the Al-Ansar cyber-terrorist forum, assisting over 4,500 users.

Irhabi007 began intelligence gathering for Al Qaeda, scouring video-sharing sites and weblogs for useful information posted on the internet by serving members of the US armed forces. He possessed videos made by a group of terrorists on a reconnaissance mission to the USA to identify possible targets. The videos included fuel-tank storage depots, the World Bank and the Capitol building.

This higher-level involvement in Al Qaeda would eventually lead to the arrest and prosecution of Irhabi007. Many anti-terrorist experts believed that Irhabi007 was an American because of his propensity to use US-based websites for hosting propaganda – and were surprised when they finally tracked down his IP address to London. But the final piece of the jigsaw puzzle was when Bosnian police arrested a group of suicide bombers who wanted to attack European targets as revenge for the invasion and occupation of Iraq and Afghanistan. When the Bosnian police examined the cell phones used by the terrorists, they found that the number of the last call made from one of them belonged to Younes Tsouli.

Irhabi007 took his cyber-terrorism seriously and used hacking techniques to compromise a large number of servers, which became hosts for Al Qaeda propaganda.

When the London police arrested Tsouli, they thought he was just another cyber-hacktivist. But as they searched through over two million computer files they realized they had caught a cyber-terrorist who was a major player in the Al Qaeda propaganda machine – Irhabi007.

As part of the Al Qaeda propaganda operation, Irhabi007 had also been setting up websites using stolen credit card numbers and false identities. But there was more to their cybercrime spree – the three cyber-terrorists had also used a huge number of phishing scams to steal credit card details. They had more than 35,000 card numbers in their possession at the time of their arrest and had acquired more than \$3.5 million (£2.25 million) from their cybercrimes. Irhabi077 had used more than 72 different stolen credit cards and false identities to pay for 80 domain names and website hosting for over 90 different web-hosting companies. The three terrorists laundered money from over 130 stolen credit cards using over 40 different online gambling sites. By using the stolen credit cards to make bets – and then collecting the winnings – the source of the money was hidden.

The terrorist cell also used their stolen credit cards to buy items such as Global Positioning (GPS) devices, night vision goggles, sleeping bags, telephones, survival knives and tents. They had purchased hundreds' of cell phones and over 250 plane tickets. All of this politically motivated cybercrime had only one aim – to support the ongoing operations of Al Qaeda and its affiliates. These cyber-terrorists had gone way beyond hacktivism and propaganda; they were actively providing material and support to the Al Qaeda network. There was nothing "virtual" about their terrorism: it had an impact in the real world.

Tsouli, Al-Daour and Mughal were all charged with conspiracy to murder, conspiracy to cause an explosion, conspiracy to cause a public nuisance, conspiracy to obtain money by deception, possession of articles promoting terrorism, and incitement to commit an act of terrorism through the internet. The evidence against them was so strong that all three pleaded guilty and were sentenced to lengthy terms in prison; Irhabi007 himself received 16 years.

This is strong evidence that cyber-terrorism has evolved. Instead of using the internet for the traditional methods of propaganda and information sharing, the internet is being actively used in intelligence gathering and long-range reconnaissance. The use of cybercrime techniques to raise funds for terrorist operations and provide long-range logistical support to active terrorist operations further blurs the line between cybercrime and cyber-terrorism. The Al Qaeda inspired cyber-terrorists have discovered social networks and are using the internet in new ways to organize and co-ordinate terrorist attacks. This is a huge change in emphasis and a worrying trend for everyone.

Cyber-terrorists are using the internet as a form of asymmetrical digital warfare that allows them to overcome their lack of numbers, their lack of funding and their lack of weapons to gain an advantage. By using the internet as a force multiplier, terrorists can amplify the apparent threat and ensure that counterinsurgency groups respond with ever harsher measures, forcing our entire internet-based society into a surveillance meltdown. When a group of cyber-terrorists can successfully confront well-financed, well-organized US cyberwar forces, we can see that the potential of the internet as a force multiplier. We have gone from "World Wide Web" to "World War Web" and there is a battle for hearts and minds being waged across the internet.

We are talking about a war of ideas in the "fifth domain". While advertising and marketing people use the internet as an effective meme spreader, cyber-warriors want to dominate cyberspace as the "fifth domain" of warfare. The militarization of the internet is underway – and cyber-terrorists are exploiting the "fifth domain" as a force multiplier in their relentless war against our society. Even now, although some of these terrorist groups no longer exist, their ideas exist on the internet. Their manifestos are everywhere and anyone can read them. The internet is a powerful force for replicating ideas, the internet is a perfect force multiplier for the digital age, where any cyber-terrorist can tap into the power of instant communication. At any point in the future the viral nature of the internet could spawn new terrorist groups that make the "Red Army Faction" (RAF) or IRA look like amateurs.

Although cyber-terrorists have colonized the internet and tapped into its power, there has never been an actual cyber-terrorist attack that compromised physical infrastructure. Until recently the cyber-terrorists have used internet as a communications device, but current developments in cyber warfare now means that cyber-terrorists could possibly attack physical infrastructure from cyberspace itself. These threats are examined in more detail in Chapter 13 (see page 131) , which looks at the possibility of a Stuxnet-like cyber weapon being unleashed and crippling an entire country.

11

CYBER-WARRIORS

If cyberwar is the "fifth domain" of warfare, then how prepared are countries across cyberspace? The primary cyber-powers in the world are the same three power blocs that have been competing for domination of the world since the cold war – the USA, Russia and China.

All three have demonstrated cyber-capabilities that make them cyber superpowers. The USA with the alleged development of Stuxnet, the Russians for their alleged use of cyber attacks as a force multiplier in the Russia-Georgia war, and the Chinese for their alleged use of cyber espionage to steal industrial secrets and software. Note the use of the word "alleged". As with all cyber attacks, the true attacker remains unknown – plausible deniability is the name of the game. There is no "smoking gun" but a growing body of evidence suggests that the major world players are gearing up for cyberwar and that there is a cyber arms race underway.

USA

The internet is a Cold War invention designed in the USA to allow communications during, and after a nuclear war, so it is no surprise that the USA have been preparing for cyberwar for many years. The USA recognizes the importance of cyberspace and wants to transform cyber warfare into a core military competence on a par with air, ground, sea and space operations. The goal is to produce a cadre of information warriors who are capable of planning and executing fully integrated cyber warfare support for traditional military operations. Such support would provide rapid network analysis to the generals in the cyberwar battle space, allowing them to choose from multiple options and to use the full range of available solutions when attacking electromagnetic, physical and human cyberwar targets.

By integrating IO into the military hierarchy, the USA hope to exploit the new opportunities of the modern techniques of cyber warfare that use rapidly developing and innovative information technologies – and which could be used to dominate the cyber-battle space. In 2003, Donald H. Rumsfeld, the US Secretary of Defense, signed the Information Operations Roadmap, which sought to advance the goal of Information Operations (IO) as a core military competency that would transform military capabilities and keep pace with emerging threats. This policy dictates that national security needs to dominate the information warfare cyber battle space while providing defence in depth against possible enemies who might take the same attitude. In order to do this the US military are constructing a complete suite of automated data analysis and decision support software tools that are designed to facilitate cyber warfare planning by combatant commanders within the cyber-battle space. Preparations for cyberwar have been underway for years, as the US military run preparedness exercises and cyberwar simulations, and it is obvious that the USA have extensive cyber warfare capabilities.

In February 2006, the US government held an exercise called Operation Cyber Storm, which included federal and state authorities as well as public and private agencies and corporations. The exercise crossed over 60 locations, five countries, and used over 700 pre-scripted messages sent via phone and email. Representatives from the governments of Australia, Canada, New Zealand and the United Kingdom were invited to observe the exercise. This cyberwar scenario specified multiple targets: internet websites, SCADA-based infrastructure, information technology, and transportation networks. The exercise simulated a large-scale cyberwar designed to infect, affect, disrupt and degrade multiple critical targets.

In the Operation Cyber Storm scenario, the attackers were assumed to be a loose coalition of cyber-hacktivists with an anti-globalization and anarchistic political agenda. In this simulation the hacktivists mounted a sophisticated and highly coordinated cyber attack across multiple targets, while also manipulating the media with false news stories to feed disinformation to the general public. The simulated cyber-hacktivists, like modern hacktivists and terrorists today, were assumed to be highly technically sophisticated – using multiple cyber attack vectors that overlapped and reinforced each other – but they were also skilled in manipulating the media by injecting false but credible stories into the news media, amplifying the apparent threat and causing disproportionate public and stock market responses. We have already seen that cyber-hacktivists and terrorists are skilled in both technical abilities and media manipulation, so the choice of simulated enemy was realistic.

The exercise highlighted several problems with the proposed US cyberwar response units. The players in the scenario found that their own methods of communication were degraded as the internet came under attack. One result of Operation Cyber Storm is that the DoHS Threat Level advisory warning now reflects the threat levels within cyberspace as well as other intelligence factors. But the most important finding was that incomplete analysis of information, or information delivered at the wrong time, is as much a problem as a complete lack of information itself. The exercise also identified that the use of disinformation during cyberwar was a big problem, and concluded that more media control (i.e. censorship) in times of crisis was important.

In 2010, the US held another full-scale cyberwar exercise that incorporated new developments in technology into the scenario. The "Cyber-shockwave" exercise went beyond Cyber Storm: it included spyware and malware that attacked and compromised smartphones; the use of botnets; and SCADA attacks on utility infrastructure. The results were startling. During the simulation over 60 million mobile phones were out of service, the SCADA attacks left 40 million people without electricity, and the Wall Street stock exchange was closed for a week. Cyber-shockwave showed that the USA was completely unprepared for a cyber attack. As the scenario unfolded, the speed of events left the participants unable to formulate a proper response. Once again the results indicated that the impact of cyberwar on the economy of a country was disproportionate to the low cost of cyberwar and the actual level of threat. The exercise theoretically showed that cyberwar would provide an asymmetrical advantage when fighting a conventional war and that the use of cyberwar was a powerful force multiplier across all military domains.

After identifying problems with the possible responses to cyberwar the USA finally integrated information warfare operations into the military. In 2010, the USA formed a new unit dedicated to cyber warfare – the United States Cyber Command (USCYBERCOM), which is designed to centralize the command of cyberspace operations, organize existing cyberwar resources and synchronize the defence of US military networks. USCYBERCOM also has an offensive role: it is prepared to conduct cyberwar operations which act as a force multiplier for the other four domains of warfare, to ensure that the USA has full spectrum domination over all of the battle space, allowing the USA freedom of action in cyberspace, while denying that freedom of action to their enemies. The US doctrine of dominating cyberspace is not unlike their military doctrine to dominate the space between the plains of Northern Germany and the borders with the USSR.

It has been alleged that the US has a budget of almost $500 billion for cyberwar research, although the official figure is $1.54 billion for the fiscal years 2013–2017.

Recent developments show that the USA has not been idle in developing an offensive cyber-weapon capability. It has been alleged that the US has a budget of almost $500 billion for cyberwar research and development, although the official figure is $1.54 billion for the fiscal years 2013–2017. Mounting evidence links the USA. The US government has not officially confirmed that it was partially responsible for the design of this cyber weapon, but two independent sources have claimed that the USA and Israel collaborated under a cyberwarfare program called Operation Olympic Games. One is alleged to be General James Cartwright, former vice-chairman to the Joint Chief of Staff, who is currently under investigation by the US government, and the second is the NSA whistle blower Edward Snowden, who has claimed asylum in Russia after being accused of espionage. This act of cyber-sabotage is alleged to have set back the Iranian nuclear program at least two years.

Finally, it should be noted that it seems likely that Stuxnet is not the only cyber weapon in the US arsenal. Speaking at a National Space Symposium in 2013, Lieutenant John Hycten suggested that the US have designated six pieces of software as cyber weapons but they have refused to name them. Some observers have suggested that this announcement was designed to trigger a cyber arms race.

We have gone from the Cold War missile gap to a **new cold war** cyber weapons gap in just a few years. The old cold war ideas of propaganda, disinformation and *maskirovka* still exist, but now the internet is both the battle space and the weapon. It is now known that the USA are preparing for offensive, rather than defensive. cyberwar and this is a major shift in US cyber-doctrine. For example, it was reported in the *New York Times* that the Obama administration in 2011 debated whether to use cyberwarfare techniques to disrupt, or disable, Libyan missile batteries by severing communications links with early warning radar. In 2013 there was a debate about whether to use cyber weaponry against Syria if the proposed armed intervention went ahead. Jason Healey, Director of the Cyber Statecraft Initiative at the Atlantic Council of the United States, advocated the use of cyber weapons against Syria.

We can reach the conclusion that cyberwar is a reality for the US, and that if cyberwar breaks out the US government will be far more concerned with protecting vital national assets such as the information infrastructure than protecting normal internet users. In times of global tension and potential cyberwar, ordinary internet users can expect web services to degrade or possibly fail altogether as large chunks of hostile internet space are blocked at a national level. If cyberwar breaks out. then the digital collateral damage could be huge.

Russia

It is widely believed by defence analysts and computer security specialists that Russia has an advanced cyberwar doctrine which emphasizes preparation and pre-strike planning, along with the known ability to carry out large-scale cyberwar attacks. The KGB was recruiting hackers for espionage purposes back in the late eighties and early nineties. Both Markus Hess and Hans Heinrich Hübner were recruited by KGB agents operating out of what was then communist-controlled East Berlin. They stole passwords, networking details and "black hat" hacking techniques and sold them to the KGB. This is the earliest known example of cyber espionage being waged across the internet. It was alleged that the Russian Federal Security service has used similar methods to the KGB and that they recruit hackers for domestic and foreign espionage. Their recruitment techniques are often coercive – i.e. "work for us or go to jail." Many Russian hackers prefer the former option to the latter.

The Russians are adept at using proxy agents such as hackers, state-controlled "youth associations" and cyber-criminals. By doing so, they gain a huge amount of plausible deniability. There is also evidence that links the cyber-criminal groups such as the Russian Business Network to the Russian government. Using proxy agents in this way reduces the risk of political fallout and the chance of retaliation by the attacked country.

Russian research on offensive software and cyber attack weapons systems designed to control the "fifth domain" are reported to be highly advanced. It was known by 2001 that Russian cyber-capabilities were extensive and the evidence today indicates that they have access to large scale botnets, viruses, worms, and automated attack tools using zero day exploits. Other cyber weapons include RATs designed to monitor communications or patch binary programs with trapdoors to enable further attacks on critical network infrastructure. The Russians have a thriving black market in counterfeit software, but this software is often modified with backdoors to allow quick and easy hostile takeover of a computer.

It is believed that in 1998 the Russians were responsible for Operation Moonlight Maze, which probed and attacked computers at the Pentagon, NASA, the Department of Energy, universities and research laboratories. During a sustained two year attack, Moonlight Maze allegedly took more than two million servers offline, and attempts were made to steal cryptographic software from a private corporation. Some of these attacks were traced back to dial-up lines from an ISP with close Russian state connections, while others emanated from a fast government internet link located in **Lab 1313** of the Russian Academy of Sciences. Military grade cryptographic software is barred from export to Russia, and one wonders why the Russians did not simply download a copy of Phil Zimmermann's Pretty Good Privacy (PGP). Perhaps the Russians already know what many hackers suspect: that the NSA can routinely crack PGP using fast supercomputers and parallel processing. The Russians, or course, denied all knowledge of the attacks, and the true identity of the attackers is unknown to this day.

However, despite official denials, there is strong evidence from translated Russian documents that there is active research into the development of cyber weapons in the following areas[12]:

- Software for disabling equipment (hard drive head resonance, monitor burnout, etc.)
- Software for erasing rewritable memory
- Software for affecting continuous power sources
- Means of penetrating information security systems
- Means of penetrating enemy information networks
- Means of concealing information collection sources
- Means of disabling all or specific software of an information system
- Means of covertly partially changing the algorithm of functioning of the software
- Means of collecting data circulating in the enemy information system
- Means of effect on data transfer protocols of communications and data transfer systems
- Means of effect on addressing and routing algorithms
- Means of intercepting and disrupting the passage of information in its technical transfer channels

We already know that the Russian government is capable of waging cyber warfare. During the Chechen conflict the Russians found that the Chechen rebels were very media savvy and proficient in using the internet to publish propaganda and disinformation supporting their cause. The Russians responded by launching denial of service attacks at the Chechen websites, even though these websites were hosted in the USA. The 2007 cyber attacks on the Estonian national infrastructure, government

12 FBIS Translation of Professor Aleksandr V. Fedorov, Russian Academy of Natural Sciences Information Weapons as a New Means of Warfare, Moscow PIR Center August 1, 2001 pp. 69-109.

websites, and internet banking websites were alleged by the Estonian government to have been perpetrated by the Russians with the express desire of destabilizing the economy. When the USA complained about the ongoing cyber attacks, the Russians denied all knowledge, instead arguing that the USA was taking a Cold War posture on information warfare in order to increase budgets and engender a "climate of fear" while engaging in a cyber arms race.

Finally, the 2008 Russia–Georgia war used cyberwar as a force multiplier to support the military conflict.[13] Prior to the beginning of the armed conflict a large number of cyber attacks were launched against Georgian government websites. The attacks included defacements of the websites of the Georgian president, the national bank and the Ministry of Foreign Affairs. This was followed up by a wave of DDoS and DoS attacks against government, education, presidential, media, banking, financial, and numerous other Georgian websites.

These cyber attacks began one day before the military offensive – a fact that led many to believe that the Russians had coordinated their cyber attacks alongside their military offensive. In total, over 147 Georgian websites were attacked during 2008 during the period 7–27 August. The Georgian government was forced to suspend all electronic banking services. This is a perfect example of an asymmetric cyber attack having far-reaching repercussions for the normal people and which damaged the economy of Georgia. The net effect was that all electronic banking services, including withdrawals from ATMs, were out of action for 10 days. The use of the cyber attacks combined with military action acted as a force multiplier for the Russian state. It meant that the chaos and confusion inflicted on the lives of normal Georgian people was almost certainly greater than the costs of the cyber attacks themselves.

Were the Russians responsible for these attacks? There were several compelling pieces of evidence suggesting Russian involvement. The botnet for the attacks had command and control servers that were tied to Russia and used the MachBot software, which is a favorite piece of software for

---

13 "Project Grey Goose: Phase I Report 17 October 2008 Russia/Georgia Cyber War – Findings and Analysis", Greylogic, 2008 / "Project Grey Goose: Phase II Report – The evolving state of cyber warfare", Greylogic, 2009

Russian botnet herders. The website, stopGeorgia.ru, which published information, hacking tutorials and malware tools for the alleged cyber-hacktivists who performed the cyber attacks, was tied to a webhosting company with alleged links to the Russian cyber-criminal underground. This website was part of a bullet-proof hosting setup designed to evade normal restrictions by using a series of mail drops, false **WHOIS** information and shell companies to prevent detection and closure.

Meanwhile, the Russian system administrators running the forums were monitoring IP traffic from the USA, but still allowing Russian nationalists in the US to take part in the strikes, further obscuring the true source of the attacks. Of course, the Russians denied all responsibility; their cyber warfare strategy openly acknowledges that part of the appeal of cyberwar is the possibility that the real source of the cyber attacks can be disguised. This is digital *maskirovka* at work again, the use of proxy agents making it impossible to determine the true attackers.

China

China has been developing cyberwar capabilities for many years. As far back as 1997, the Chinese created a virus-research unit, and they created a specialized hacking unit in 1999. In 1998, the Red Hacker Alliance was formed as a response to political tension between Indonesia and China. This led to the emergence of informal groupings of Chinese nationalist hackers who attacked targets perceived to be anti-Chinese. Between 1995 and 2005, the Red Hacker Alliance affiliated with other Chinese hacker groups such as China Eagle, Javaphile and the group known as Ultra-Right Wing Chinese Hackers Opposed to Japanese Alliance. The infamous "Honker Union of China" was formed in 2000, and in 2001, the Honker Union of China declared a seven day cyberwar to protest against the Hainan Island incident, where the a midair collision with a US aircraft allegedly involved in surveillance lead to the death of the pilot Wang Wei. The cyberwar was finally called off, but not before the hackers compromised and defaced more than 1,000 websites. The Red Hacker Alliance was a large hacking group that owned around 250 websites and hacker forums. The entire membership of the informal groups affiliated with Red Hacker Alliance was estimated to be approximately 300,000.

Unlike other Chinese hacker groups such as Blue Hackers or Black Hackers, who more closely resemble the western hacking scene, the Red Hacker Alliance was imbued with a fervent sense of Chinese nationalism. Eventually the Red Hacker Alliance appeared to disband and mutate into the Chinese hacking underground, but many security experts doubt that this is really the case. It appears that the Chinese have access to a skilled technical cadre built on the foundations of the 300,000 hackers who were part of the Red Hacker Alliance – technical experts with the skills and the motivation to wage cyberwar. Are the Chinese hackers truly independent or are they tools of the Chinese government? It seems strange that a country that suppresses opposition to the government and censors the internet allows the hacker sub-culture to flourish at all. It has been surmised that the activities of the hackers are tolerated as long as the subjects of the attacks are not Chinese websites – anything else is fair game.

Over the last few years there has been a growing body of evidence that China is heavily involved in cyber espionage. China, of course, deny being behind the attacks, but the targets are often high-value political, economic, diplomatic or military targets – all containing strategic information valuable to the Chinese military industrial complex. Here are a few recent examples that suggest Chinese involvement in cyber espionage.

Operation Aurora

During 2009, Google and a large number of other US companies had their computers compromised and data stolen. Google later alleged that the purpose of the attack was to compromise the Gmail accounts of Chinese dissidents and monitor their email communications, but some observers have suggested that the attackers managed to steal the Google "crown jewels" – the source code used by Google itself. The list of compromised computers included some of the top US technology companies: Rackspace, Adobe Systems, Juniper Networks, Google, Yahoo, Symantec, Morgan Stanley and Dow Chemicals were amongst the 20 companies allegedly penetrated.

What is the evidence that the Chinese were behind the attacks? Operation Aurora used the "Hydraq" malware, which is the Chinese black hat weapon of choice for cyber espionage. Hydraq is a sophisticated RAT that allows the attacker full hostile takeover of the target computer, monitoring of communications and remote controlled data theft. Attribution for Operation Aurora was difficult, as the command and control computers for the RATs were based in Taiwan, but since the targets were all US high-tech companies many security analysts came to the conclusion that Operation Aurora was Chinese in origin. Some experts have alleged that the origin of the attacks was Shanghai Jiao Tong University and the Lanxiang Vocational School in China, both of which have links to the Chinese state apparatus. The Chinese, of course, have denied all involvement in the attacks, claiming that the alleged cyber espionage incident was "part of a US government conspiracy".

Operation GhostNet

In 2008, the Information Warfare Monitor undertook an investigation into allegations that the computers and networks of the Dalai Lama and the Tibetan Government in Exile were infected with malware. The investigators were shocked at what they found – over 1,200 computers in 100 different countries were infected by a RAT called "Gh0st Rat" and other malware. Gh0st Rat – like Hydraq – is designed for cyber espionage and data exfiltration, rather than standard trojans used by cyber-criminals for monetary gain.

The primary source of infection was a spear phishing attack purporting to come from campaigns@freetibet.org, which contained an infected word file. When the document was opened, it appeared normal but in the background it silently installed malware onto the computer. Once installed the Gh0st Rat trojan took total control of the computer and registered with one of the command and control servers – the majority of which were based in mainland China. Although command and control servers have been discovered in other countries, it appears that the malware uses the same encryption key, indicating a single point of origin and command and control.

It appears that the computers targeted were highly specific – over 30 per cent of the compromised computers would have been considered high-value targets containing information valuable to the Chinese. The RAT enabled the attackers to steal a large number of private documents, including important policy documents from the Dalai Lama. Once again, the Chinese denied being behind the attacks.

Operation ShadowNet

After the conclusion of the GhostNet investigation, the Information Warfare Monitor group continued their research and discovered another botnet engaged in cyber espionage, which had suspicious links to China. They eventually named the new botnet ShadowNet, and it was found to be targeted on Indian government interests. Once the botnet was analyzed it was found that over 40 per cent of the infected computers were located in India. Indian embassies in Belgium, Serbia, Germany, Italy, Kuwait and the USA were compromised.

It was soon discovered that the botnet communicated with a command and control server in China. In fact, the core group of command and control servers – nearly a dozen in all – were also located in China. At least one of the people involved in running the ShadowNet botnet was a known Chinese hacker with links to Chinese hacker groups. When the Information Warfare Monitor team tracked down the command and control servers of ShadowNet they retrieved a number of stolen documents. Over 90 per cent of the stolen documents were from computers located in India – including documents marked as SECRET, RESTRICTED and CONFIDENTIAL.

Once again we have evidence that indicates a highly targeted cyber espionage attack against India, with the subsequent theft of a large number of documents of strategic interest to a single country – China. Once again China has denied all involvement in this incident of cyber espionage.

Examination of these three cyber espionage incidents – Aurora, GhostNet and ShadowNet – shows a pattern that is highly suggestive of Chinese involvement. But are the attacks nothing more than cyber-terrorism carried out by nationalist hacktivists, as the Chinese government would have us believe?

It seems strange that so many incidents of computer espionage should be linked to China. Each attack benefits Chinese strategic interests, and have strong links to Chinese web hosting sites – including web-hosting sites close to Chinese military interests. All of the software used is software that the Chinese hackers prefer and is written in Chinese. Manuals for a RAT were found and were in Chinese. The software itself contains Chinese help messages.

The weight of evidence suggests Chinese government involvement but no conclusive proof. The repeated denials by China also obfuscate the true origin of the attacks. It has been suggested by some computer cyber warfare experts that Russia uses a form of digital *maskirovka* and that it writes malware in Chinese to further contribute to the fog of cyberwar. Did the Russians subvert computers in China and write their malware in Chinese to lay the blame for the current spate of cyber espionage on China? The use of plausible deniability might be essential in waging covert digital warfare, but now there is a possible "smoking gun" that links a unit in Chinese People's Liberation Army (PLA) to at least some of the cyber espionage attacks.

> ... the software the hackers prefer is written in Chinese. Manuals for a RAT were found and were in Chinese. The software itself contains Chinese help messages.

The cyber-security company Mandiant claims to have identified the actors behind some of the wave of cyber espionage as being both Chinese and state-sponsored. By observing attacks over a period of two years, the investigators determined that 98 per cent of all the attacks were from internet addresses in China and that 97 per cent of the remote desktop sessions were using the Chinese language keyboard settings. The security experts determined that the attacks were originating from four networks in Shanghai – two of which are in the Pudong New Area.

Is it a coincidence, then, that the PLA military networking operations unit is situated in the Pudong New Area? The mission of **Unit 61398** is to conduct military-grade network operations – or, in other words, cyberwar. Unit 61398 recruits talented technical experts with experience in covert communications, English language skills, operating system internals, digital signal processing and network security. It is estimated to have hundreds, if not thousands of staff, and is served by a high-speed fiber optic communications network. Is Unit 61398 behind some of the cyber espionage attacks? The weight of evidence suggests that it is, but as Mandiant[4] wryly suggests, there is another unlikely possibility:

> "A secret, resourced organization full of mainland Chinese speakers with direct access to Shanghai-based telecommunications infrastructure is engaged in a multi-year, enterprise scale computer espionage campaign right outside of Unit 61398's gates, performing tasks similar to Unit 61398's known mission."[14]

The increasing body of evidence that indicates China is an emerging cyberwar threat cannot be ignored. But the Chinese are as adept at digital *maskirovka* as their Russian counterparts. By tolerating the nationalist underground hacking groups, such as the Red Hacker Alliance, the Chinese government has an effective smokescreen to mask state-sponsored attacks. The use of proxy agents in this way adds to the cyber "fog of war" and makes it impossible for the country being attacked to attribute the attacks directly to China.

Meanwhile, the Chinese government have issued strong denials, claiming that the Mandiant report lacks firm evidence to link the IP addresses used by Unit 61398 with the IP addresses used in the attacks, and that IP addresses are "often hijacked by hackers". The Chinese media meanwhile have called the report "groundless" and "irresponsible", alleging that the Mandiant report "reeks of a commercial stunt", and have accused US politicians and businessmen of hyping a Chinese hacker threat for their own interests. The USA have taken the Mandiant report seriously enough that the problem of cyber espionage originating from China has reached the political agenda, with Barack Obama claiming to have engaged in "tough talk" and insisting that he expects China to "follow international norms and abide by international rules".

If the three largest power blocs in the world are preparing for cyberwar, what about other countries?

14 "Shadows in the Cloud: Investigating Cyber Espionage 2.0", Joint Report JR03-2010, Information Warfare Monitor/Shadowserver Foundation, 2010

UK

The UK has been late in waking up to the ongoing cyberwars but is planning to catch up fast. By 2013 it became apparent that the UK was under cyber attack and that **Government Communications Headquarters (GCHQ)** blamed the Chinese and Russians for these attacks. As a result it was announced that the UK was developing a cyber warfare capability. Defence Secretary Philip Hammond said, "Last year our cyber defences blocked around 400,000 advanced malicious cyber threats against the government's secure intranet alone" and added that "simply building cyber defences is not enough: as in other domains of warfare, we also have to deter. Britain will build a dedicated capability to counter attack in cyberspace and if necessary to strike in cyberspace." In response to the imminent threat of cyberwar, the UK Ministry of Defence is planning to create a new Joint Cyber Reserve Unit and recruit hundreds of computer experts to work with regular military forces. However the problem is that there are not enough computer hackers available, and there has been proposals to recruit convicted hackers into the newly formed cyber strike force. The close links between the NSA and Government Headquarters (GCHQ) allow the UK to tap into American expertise in cyber warfare techniques. In the wake of the Snowden revelations, media reports have alleged that GCHQ and the NSA are actively developing cyber weapons together, but currently no details about the type of cyber weapons have been released. The current UK budget allocated to cyber warfare will rise to £650 million over the next four years. This, on top of the estimated £1.7 million allocated to GCHQ for surveillance purposes, and the money received from the NSA – £22.9 million ($36m) in 2009, and £39million ($61m) in 2010. It seems that the UK is finally taking the possibility of cyber warfare seriously.

The "special relationship" with the USA and UK could be an Achilles heel for the UK cyberwar effort. Can the UK really trust cyber weapons and encryption technology supplied by the NSA, who have a reputation for subverting encryption algorithms? Can the NSA be trusted to supply 100 per cent secure software to the UK? Or will they leverage the "special relationship" to infiltrate UK computer systems?

The use of advanced cyberwar techniques by the NSA, and we know that they have them, could be used to subvert the entire networking system of the UK, and we would not even know it. Defence in depth is the key, and that includes defence against possible digital collateral damage caused by allies in time of cyberwar. Therefore, it is even more important that the UK formulates a proper cyber-response plan and a proper cyber warfare doctrine that allows cyber-warriors to be integrated into the MoD, rather than organizations which have close links to the USA, like the GCHQ. More important than the technical agenda, the UK needs a political agenda, so that they have both the will to do and the ability to do without being reduced to acting as proxy agents of the US cyber-power hegemony.

India and Pakistan

The ongoing cyber-skirmishes between India and Pakistan should not be underestimated. They may be the precursor to cyberwar between the two nations. The situation between India and Pakistan has long been difficult. The festering wound of Kashmir has led to both military action and diplomatic sabre rattling that has sometimes broken out into open warfare across the Line of Control (LOC) guarded by both sides. The situation is not helped by the fact that both sides have nuclear weapons, and that the Pakistani nukes are often referred to as The Islamic Bomb. As elsewhere, clashes between Indian and Pakistani cyber-hacktivists normally occur at time of political stress. But recent developments suggest that both sides are now taking cyberwar seriously and incorporating it into their conventional military doctrine.

The loose-knit cyber-hactivist collective Pakistan Cyber-army (PCA) is one of the best known groups waging cyberwar against India, but there are others including Team_H4tr!cK, Pakistan Hackers Club and "Pakistan G–Force". Since 1989 these groups have been waging low-level cyberwar against the Indian government, usually defacing Indian websites. The number and frequency of the attacks are rising: there were 217 in 2007 and by 2011[1] there were allegedly over 1000 attacks by cyber-hacktivists on Indian websites. More troubling is the fact that Pakistani hacktivists have possibly penetrated the Bhabha Atomic Research Centre (BARC) website and stolen user details such as names, email addresses and phone numbers. The PCA don't just attack India. In 2012 they hacked and defaced over 400 websites in China and Bangladesh.

The PCA are also skilled at using social media and have their own Facebook page, where they brag that they have "knocked down" over 20,000 Indian websites in the last few years. The same page also details attacks on Israeli websites.

We can conclude that Pakistani hackers are no strangers to the other level of cyber warfare, where the fifth domain of cyberwar collides with the fifth domain of propaganda, advertising and marketing. The same online tools used to promote the cyber-economy can be subverted and re-purposed in the hands of skilled cyberhacktivists who use digital psychological operations (PSYOPS) to spread disinformation across a large population.

Fake images can be amusing, but in the hands of cyber-hacktivists such as the PCA they are a deadly weapon of mass media destruction.

The 2012 attacks by the PCA went much further than the normal web defacements used in normal cyber-hacktivist skirmishes. By using internet websites and social media, the PCA were able to use disinformation to spread fear across cyberspace, which then affected the general population. This a perfect example of digital psychological operations (PSYOPS) to cause fear and confusion in the enemy population, using the internet as a force multiplier.

Firstly, the cyber-hacktivists recycled images of violence and disasters from a large number of countries. These images were faked up using digital image manipulation to become "faux-tography". Fake images, which circulate the internet on a daily basis, can be amusing, but in the hands of cyber-hacktivists such as the PCA they are a deadly weapon of mass media destruction. The pictures suggested that the images were of atrocities against Muslim Indians from the "other community" i.e. the Hindu Indians. The pictures were uploaded to a variety of social media websites. The next step was to create chaos and confusion by using a crowdsourced group of hacktivists to send SMS messages to people close to the border in Assam. When the population took the bait, there was a mass movement of nearly half a million Indians, who believed that the rumors were true. When the Indian government protested that a sleeper group of cyber-hacktivists acting on behalf of the Pakistani ISI were behind the disinformation campaign, the government of Pakistan denied all knowledge of the alleged cyber attacks.

In response to these types of attacks, a group who call themselves the Indian Cyber Army have been busy attacking Pakistani cyber-assets since 2008. In 2010, they hacked a server hosting a number of websites and defaced the websites belonging to the Pakistan Army and the Ministry of Foreign Affairs, Ministry of Education, Ministry of Finance, Pakistan Computer Bureau and Council of Islamic Ideology. In total, 36 Pakistani websites were defaced, allegedly in response to the terrorist attacks in Mumbai in 2008. On the second anniversary of the Mumbai attacks in 2010 the Indian Cyber Army claimed to have attacked 870 Pakistani websites including the State Bank of Pakistan. Pakistani authorities alleged that the attacks carried out by the Indian Cyber Army were, in reality, planned and coordinated by the Indian National Technical Research Organization (NTRO). The Indians, of course, denied all knowledge of the attacks.

> On the second anniversary of the Mumbai attacks in 2010 the Indian Cyber Army claimed to have attacked 870 Pakistani websites, including the State Bank of Pakistan.

By 2013, a group of Norwegian cyber-security experts, claimed to have located an Indian cyber espionage ring similar to those allegedly used by China. Operation Hangover, as the cyber-experts named it, have been running for at least three years and exfiltrating documents affecting Indian national security policy.[12] The Indian hacktivists used typical phishing techniques to exploit computer vulnerabilities to install RATs and steal sensitive data. The report concluded that there was no evidence that the Indian government was involved, but suggested that a known group of nationalist hackers were responsible. Either way the data was stolen, and it is hard to see what use a hacker would make of data related to Indian national security. Where did the data go? The current cyberwars between Pakistani and India are very typical of this low level form of covert digital warfare. But, as we have seen, there is a fine line between "nationalist hacktivists" and the use of proxy agents by governments.

Military experts in India have demanded that India updates its cyber forces. They have also called for a military doctrine that includes both defensive measures to protect computers, smartphones, networks and vital infrastructure, but to also use offensive measures to launch a cyber attack on any potential enemy. Given the high level of technological literacy in India, they could potentially raise one of the largest cyber-armies in the world.

Are the Indians preparing for cyberwar? The answer is yes. The Indian Government budgeted $7.76 million (£4.8million) in 2012–13 for cyber-security, and have set up a National Cyber Command to protect Indian cyberspace. In 2009, the Indian army conducted a readiness exercise called Divine Matrix. It included a simulation of a nuclear attack by China, which was preceded by a cyber attack. The Chinese, needless to say, were not happy with this cyberwar readiness exercise. The spokesman for the Foreign Ministry, Qin Gang, said of the cyber warfare exercise, "Leaders of China and India had already reached a consensus that the two countries will not pose a threat to each other but rather treat each other as partners." But, as we have seen, there is strong evidence that the Chinese military and nationalist hackers have been waging a low-level cyberwar using cyber espionage against Indian diplomatic and industry assets. When the evidence is so overwhelming, the Indians can hardly be blamed for stepping up their cyber warfare and cyber-intelligence programs against the Chinese and Pakistanis.

The Indian nation is in a very good condition to wage a successful cyberwar. The technological infrastructure in large cities such as Bangalore is world class. Indians have been exploiting this technology for many years, and large numbers of US and UK corporations outsource IT such as helpdesks to the Indian subcontinent. There is a huge potential cadre of programmers and hackers in India, both in academia and the private sector. This experience is vital for Indian cyber warfare preparations to succeed.

The close proximity to Pakistan means that India has some unlikely allies. Recent evidence suggests that India is receiving help from Israel in their development of cyber warfare capabilities. Experts have reported that within the cyber warfare division of the Israeli military, a cyber-division has been developed to wage cyberwar against Pakistan and Islamic militant cyber-hacktivists. The reported budget for this is around $15 million (£9.3 million). The intention: to perform acts of cyber espionage, information gathering and other cyber-operations against the government of Pakistan. Is the Israel Defense Forces' Military Intelligence **Unit 8200**, who were alleged to have helped in the development of the Stuxnet worm, now working against Pakistani strategic interests? What we do know, is that the Iranian uranium enrichment program used the crude AR1 centrifuges designed by AQ Khan, the "father" of the Pakistani atomic bomb. Does the Pakistani government still use that type of centrifuge? Are they still monitored by Siemens' based SCADA systems? If so, a cyber attack using Stuxnet, or some variant thereof, is very likely. It would benefit both India and Israel to perform covert acts of cyber-sabotage on the Pakistani nuclear program. It would benefit them even more if the acts of cyber-sabotage were traced back to a third party such as China. Once again the use of plausible deniability acts as a force multiplier in cyber warfare.

> After the 2013 attack on the Washington Post and The New York Times, the Syrian Electronic Army hacked an Associated Press Twitter account to spread false rumors that caused a temporary dip in the stock market.

The rest of the world is also preparing itself for cyberwar. We can see that nationalist cyber-hacktivists are involved in cyber-skirmishes that amount to a low level of cyber warfare. The "brush fire" wars between India and Pakistan, which has been ongoing since 1989; the electronic intifada against Israel by pro-Palestinian cyber-hacktivists; the Russia–Georgia cyberwar of 2008 and the claims of cyber espionage levelled against China between 2008–2013 all are a sign of things to come. In Syria, the Syrian Electronic Army, the allegedly "independent" hacktivist group, has been accused of being an arm of the Syrian government. After the 2013 attack on the *Washington Post* and *The New York Times*, the Syrian Electronic Army hacked an Associated Press Twitter account to spread false rumors that caused a temporary dip in the stock market. Because of this, the FBI has now classified the Syrian Electronic Army as a terrorist organization.

Iran

The Stuxnet attack in 2010 caught the Iranians off guard, but Iran has now beefed up its preparations for cyberwar and started a development program for cyber weapons of its own. It has offensive plans that include cyber attacks against specific government websites and critical infrastructure. The Iranians are believed to have an arsenal of cyber weapons that include viruses, worms, and RATs. The current estimated Iranian budget for cyber warfare is $76 million ($46 million). Some experts argue that Iranian cyber weapons are relatively unsophisticated and describe Iran as a Tier Three cyber-power, but suggest that those weapons could damage US infrastructure and communications. It is unlikely that Iran have the capability to attack US military interests directly, but as the 2008 Russia–Georgia cyberwar showed, even a limited cyberwar attacking banks and government websites can have a huge impact on the economy of a country.

Israel

Israel is no stranger to covert warfare and the use of terrorism and counter-terrorism to gain a strategic advantage. It is widely believed that the Israeli intelligence services, including MOSSAD, are some of the most effective in the world. Therefore it should come as no surprise that Israel has long been using techniques of information warfare and cyberwar in its intelligence and military operations. The Israeli Defense Force (IDF) Military Intelligence Unit 8200, known for its advanced signal intelligence capabilities, is almost certainly the central core of cyberwar operations in Israel. Some experts suspect that it was Unit 8200 which collaborated with the USA in the creation of the Stuxnet worm.

But Israel has been involved in "brush fire" cyberwars with cyber-hacktivists and terrorists for some time. There has been a digital covert war between Israeli cyber-hacktivists and their Islamic counterparts for many years.

The standard method of Israeli hacktivists was to block channels of online communication such as Al Jazeera, the Hamas website, or other

Islamic websites. They normally used a simple DDoS attack, which overloaded and crashed the web server. The Israeli hackers are familiar with plausible deniability and they often use compromised computers in other countries to hide the true source of the attack. They are also known to use botnets to accomplish these attacks. It is not known if the botnets used in these attacks are Israeli in origin, or are just hired from botnet herders in the cyber-criminal underground. In a form of digital escalation, a loose alliance of Islamic hacktivists called "Unity" announced that a "four-phase cyberwar" would be carried out against Israel and its allies.

Phase One

Crash official government Israeli websites

Phase Two

Attack commercial targets i.e., the Bank of Israel, and Tel Aviv stock market

Phase Three

Attack the Israeli ISP infrastructure e.g. servers and routers

Phase Four

The destruction of Israeli e-commerce sites

The group claimed to be able to shut down 70 per cent of Israeli internet traffic. They also warned "this is not just a war against Israel, but also against the USA", and threatened to use the same four-phase war plan to launch cyber attacks against the USA. Whilst they claimed that they could knock out 70 per cent of Israeli internet infrastructure, they never came close to accomplishing their threat. One reason could be that Phase Three – the destruction of the Israeli internet infrastructure – blocks the goal of Phase Four – the destruction of e-commerce. As has been pointed out already, in a cyberwar the last thing to be destroyed will be the internet, because while it is both the method and vector of cyber attack, in cyberwar, *the internet is the weapon.*

Close links with the USA, a large cadre of technically skilled cyber-hacktivists and the existence of Unit 8200 implies that Israel is taking cyberwar seriously, and their preparations for cyberwar has led them to be been rated by many experts[15] one of the top global cyber-powers in the world.

North Korea and South Korea

The South Koreans have alleged for many years that the North Korean government runs a training school to produce a "secret army of hackers". North Korea's cyberwar assets are said to include the possibility of damaging the command and control structure of the Pacific fleet and the possibility of a SCADA attack on the power grid of the US mainland. The USA took these claims seriously enough to hold a cyberwar exercise called Eligible Receiver 97 in June 1997. Experts from the NSA used nearly 2,000 hacking tools available for download on the internet. The cyber-warriors attacked unclassified Department of Defense computers and parts of the critical national infrastructure. The results of the exercise showed that such an attack was possible and could have disrupted the command systems of the Pacific fleet based in Honolulu, while also taking control of power grid infrastructure.

South Korea is an ideal target for cyberwar. It has a high-speed internet connection nationwide for hi-tech research purposes, and it is a highly connected country, with over 41 million internet users and eight million ADSL connections. Such a huge attack surface combined with high-speed connections to the internet means that a full scale cyber attack could take control of the majority of the networking infrastructure of the country. This could then provide a platform for further attacks against the USA or other enemies that could be attributed to South Korea. The USA took this risk seriously enough to mount a joint US-Korean exercise. The 2008 Ulchi Freedom Guardian military exercise included a scenario called Infocon, which simulated a massive attack on the South Korean networks using hacking and virus attacks.

15 John Leyden, "Cyberwar report: Israel, Finland best prepared for conflict", 2012, *The Register*

In September 2013 the South Koreans accused North Korea of cyber espionage. In a period of heightened political tensions after North Korea carried out its third nuclear test and threatened attacks on neighboring countries, a group of North Korean hackers used spear phishing to infect South Korean computers with a RAT. This program was designed to steal text documents in the format used by the word processor used widely by the South Korean government. Computer security experts described the Kimsuky RAT as unsophisticated, but it was capable of performing a hostile takeover, spy on the user and exfiltrate documents.

Several months earlier in March 2013, there was a major cyber attack on South Korea, which affected over 48,000 computers and servers in South Korea. Some banks were unable to function for up to five days, although the banks deny that personal data was compromised. Reporters at the major TV stations were unable to log into their computer systems for several days. When security experts examined the malware used in the attacks, they found that 30 of the 76 pieces of malware used in the attack were recycled from an earlier cyber attack attributed to North Korea. There was also further evidence inside the malware: the path to the directory containing the source code was found to have Korean characters, which when translated were the words "attack" and "completion". Strong evidence again – but no smoking gun, and the North Koreans have denied all knowledge of the attacks.

Conclusion

We now know that at least 120 countries are preparing for cyberwar, including Brazil, Canada, France, Germany, Italy and Netherlands, but more surprisingly, several African states such as Kenya, Nigeria and South Africa. Who are the most dangerous countries in the ongoing cyberwars? We can evaluate them on several levels: Do they have a cadre of "black hat" programmers? Do they have a budget for development of cyber weapons? Are they running cyber military exercises to prepare for cyber war?

Tier One

These are the big power blocs of the "old Cold War", but they are also technologically advanced and have a large population of hackers. It is no coincidence that the USA, Russia and China have the highest level cyberwar capabilities. The USA has the edge, because their computer scientists invented the internet, and their early start in networking communications means that 86% of the entire bandwidth of the globe flows through satellite, fiber and other media through internet hubs that the US control. It can be argued that China does not have the capability of waging an offensive cyber-war, because it has demonstrated only its cyber-espionage capabilities. The evidence from the GhostNet (2008) and ShadowNet (2010) incidents suggests that the Chinese are capable of sophisticated penetrations of any computer, wherever it is. Meanwhile, the emergence of an Islamic cyber-bloc is an interesting development. It uses crowdsourcing to promote both cyber-hacktivism and cyber-terrorism. For cyber-hacktivists the internet is used for spreading propaganda and mounting cyber attacks and is a force multiplier that allows cyber-hacktivists to have a high impact despite their low numbers.

Tier Two

Proxy states are the key to cyber war. The Tier Two cyber war capabilities are mostly in countries that are aligned with one, or possibly more, Tier One state actors. This includes Pakistan, India, North Korea and South Korea, among many others. There is evidence that all of the Tier One nation state actors are actively seeking partnerships with proxy states by sharing technology and possible developments in cyber-weaponry – for example, the US and Israel work with India. These Tier Two cyber-powers have the capability to wage limited cyber-warfare and espionage, but as yet have not developed an offensive cyber weapons capability along the lines of Stuxnet, but this is just a matter of time.

Tier Three

The rest of the world is gearing up for cyberwar. For many years the UK did not even have a military and political doctrine defining cyberwar. These "also-rans" need to invest more in cyber warfare, or buy a cyber weapon from a supplier. With the USA leading the field, and Russia and China not far behind, there is a new cyber-arms race developing, which threatens everybody on the internet. The USA's NSA have knowledge of zero day vulnerabilities before the general public do, because the vendors share them with the government, but the evidence suggests that the NSA are also buying zero day vulnerabilities on the black market.

All the evidence presented in this chapter suggests that we are in the middle of a cyber-arms race. Spending on cyber-defence has accelerated over the past decade across the globe. The growth of the "military industrial information complex" means that any country can now purchase cyber weapons on the open market. Spending on cyber-offence – the money spent on research and development of cyber weapons which have the potential to destroy critical infrastructure of a country, has also increased. The 2013 Visiongain report has estmated that the annual global cyber-warfare market will be as high as $16.96 billion (£10.6 billion) in 2013. It is no longer necessary to develop a cadre of programmers with technical expertise, and now any country with the cash can begin to purchase a cyber-warfare capability.

If history is any guide, this suggests that the military information complex will soon be earning vast amounts of tax payer money as corporations with military contracts revamp, rehash, and recycle the malware, rootkits and RATs available on the internet.

The ongoing cyberwars don't just represent a threat to our computers, but also our wallets, as cyber-warfare budgets could become hugely inflated. Despite the opinions of many computer security experts, cyberwar is a reality now, and a new cyber-arms race is under way. Modern technology is available to fuel an arms race of this magnitude, and now countries across the globe have the will to do it. As history teaches us, once an arms race is underway, a war is almost inevitable. The current cyber-arms race is no different, and it makes our collective digital futures more uncertain and more dangerous. It seems that cyberwar has crossed the boundaries of science fiction and become science fact, and we must conclude that full-scale global cyberwar is inevitable.

12

CYBER WEAPONS

The concept of a cyber weapon is as difficult to define as cyberspace itself. What is a cyber weapon? The truth is, cyber weapons are everywhere andit is this availability that represents the first level of cyber weapon threat.

The tools provided with your computer operating system can be used by a skilled hacker or cyber-warrior to explore, test and maybe exploit security vulnerabilities. Some Linux installations provide network testing and exploration tools that are classed as dual use tools. In the hands of a security expert they are useful for securing a network. In the hands of a hacker or cyber warrior, they can be used to subvert the network. Network monitoring tools designed to monitor the state of the network can be used to watch login interactions across an unencrypted internet connection in real time. Many of these dual use tools of this sort now show up on anti-malware scans as possible hacking tools. If you don't use them, then you should think about deleting them. But your computer itself can be subverted – compromised, infected and subject to hostile takeover by a RAT or botnet client. Once compromised, your computer becomes a cyber weapon without your knowledge – a part of covert digital wars raging across the internet.

The second level of cyber weapon threat is the tool that can be downloaded for computer security purposes and then abused to compromise networks and computers. This is the software that is designed for only one purpose, to allow the skilled operator to test and penetrate system security. In the wrong hands, however, they are the internet equivalent of the AK–47 assault rifle: easy to acquire, cheap to own and very reliable.

Network and computer scanning utilities are the commonest type of software that fall into this category. Thinking about Nmap as a purpose-built program designed to scan networks and multiple computers for vulnerabilities, as opposed to thinking about it as a possible cyber weapon, is just a question of attitude and motivation. Vulnerability scanners such as Nessus are designed to seek and find computers with security holes, while penetration testing engines such as MetaSploit can then subvert the integrity of the target computer. This is the grey area of dual use tools and cyber weapons, as much of this software can be used for both good and evil, but still have a useful function within the computer security world. Entire Linux distributions loaded with cyber attack software are easily available for download from the internet. Using system security distributions of this type requires a level of technical expertise that many users do not have, but in the wrong hands can wreak havoc.

There is no doubt about the third level of cyber weapon: evil malware designed only to exploit and infect other computers. Illegal malware such as RATs, spyware and botnet clients are everywhere on the internet and maybe on your computer also. The problem with this level of malware and crime-ware is that anyone with the cash can buy it. Anyone can decompile, recompile, modify and recycle an executable program. But worse still, there are large amounts of source code available on the web. Once the techniques embedded inside the malware are available to all, then those attacks multiply across the web at the speed of light.

It is now known that the National Security Agency (NSA) has access to Microsoft's zero day vulnerabilities long before the fix arrives on Patch Tuesday. That window of opportunity allows cyber-warriors to write cyber attack tools using those zero day vulnerabilities, long before Microsoft writes a security fix. It is also well known that malware writers – including cyber-terrorists and cyber-criminals track Patch Tuesday. Once the patch is issued, they reverse-engineer the patch code, dig deep into the operating system to find the vulnerability, and then write an exploit. With the average computer remaining unpatched for over 30 days, this gives both cyber-warriors and evil malware writers plenty of time to compromise thousands of computers attached to the internet.

The fourth and final level of cyber weapons are the purpose-built tools that are developed covertly by nation states such as the USA, Russia and China with the express intention of waging cyber warfare on another country. Some countries recycle known malware to compromise computers because it makes an easy route to plausible deniability. If the tools are known to be used by cyber-criminals and hackers, any government can deny all knowledge of the attacks especially if mounted from a computer in another country. Hackers tend to use tools in their own languages – making attribution easy – but (as discussed elsewhere) some countries actively engaged in cyber warfare, Russia as one example, actuwrite code in foreign languages, notably Chinese, to make investigation and attribution more difficult.

This is digital *maskirovka* at work. Writing code in Chinese, basing the attacks from servers in the Chinese sphere of influence and then reaping the benefits while the political and diplomatic blowback falls on China is a masterpiece of cyber warfare planning. The true art of covert digital warfare is made apparent in an instant: stealth, doubtful attribution and a lack of collateral cyber-damage are the key to the deployment of a successful cyber weapon.

> **Some countries actively engaged in cyber warfare, actually write code in foreign languages, notably Chinese, to make attribution more difficult.**

This is at the heart of the cyber weapon debate. The cyber weapons are inside your computer and your computer itself can become a cyber weapon. But the most powerful cyber weapons are being built by nation state actors in an ongoing cyber arms race. How does a country respond to an act of cyberwar as opposed to an act of war? Nobody knows. The rules of engagement for normal warfare are well understood, but cyberwar, the new covert digital warfare of the fifth domain, is unknown territory. Nobody can agree on what a cyber weapon is and even the US government will not tell us. A recent announcement by the USA government outlining six pieces of malware that were now classed as cyber weapons did not clear the fog of cyberwar – rather, it enhanced it – as they refused to name the hacking tools that have become cyber weapons.

Italian cyber-security and cyber warfare expert Stefano Mele defines a cyber weapon as a "device or any set of computer instructions intended to unlawfully damage a system acting as a critical infrastructure, its information, the data or programs therein contained or therefore relevant, or even facilitate the interruption, total or partial, or alteration of its operation". This is as good as it gets – including devices as well as computer code itself. Cyber weapons can just be computer code, but physical devices such as cell phone jammers, or even Electro Magnetic Pulse (EMP) weapons are also cyber weapons when used against critical infrastructure. [16]

Stuxnet: The first "Cyber Weapon"?

To understand why the Stuxnet worm was an important incident in the history of cyber warfare ,a little history is needed. Once upon a time hackers wrote malware called a "virus". The early viruses were very simple:they infected the boot-block of a computer so that every floppy disk inserted into that computer became infected with a new copy of the virus. The evolution of early viruses led to more sophisticated versions. Now when they copied themselves they attached themselves to the computer code of programs, the "executables". When the executable program was invoked, it would seek to infect the boot-block of the floppy disk or other program files.

These days anti-virus software is everywhere – trying to protect us against all manner of viruses – but it cannot protect us against a computer "worm". The difference between a "worm" and "virus" is simple. A worm does not need to be propagated across floppy disks. A modern computer worm is a sophisticated package of cyber attack code designed to live in cyberspace, to explore the local area network or the internet and find new hosts to infect. Once infected the new hosts then explore their network and infect more hosts. Worms are viruses with enough intelligence to seek out computers across cyberspace which are vulnerable.

It wasn't always like this. In the early days of computing, many researchers speculated that a proper worm could run through the network to fix problems, rather than cause them. This line of thought came to a grinding halt after the infamous internet worm of 1988 crippled the proto-internet. The worm used several security exploits

16 Stefano Mele, "Cyber weapons: legal and strategic aspects Version 2.0", 2013, Italian Institute of Strategic Studies

within the UNIX system and managed to compromise over 6,000 computers before being stopped. The author of the worm, Robert Tappan Morris (RTM), was prosecuted and fined $10,050 (£6,500), given three years probation and 400 hours community service. Conspiracy theorists find it interesting that the father of RTM was an NSA cryptologist who specialized in computers – but no smoking gun linking the NSA to the internet worm has ever been found. Many computer scientists interested in writing good worms lost interest in the field after the internet worm disaster, but RTM's line of research did not stop for the malware writers. The cat was out of the bag and over the next few years many more worms appeared, each more sophisticated than the last and more dangerous and more widespread.

Computer worms are an Advanced Persistent Threat (APT) – advanced because they can infect many computers very quickly using the zero day exploits in the attack package and persistent because they can lie dormant for long periods and use stealth methods such as rootkits to avoid detection and removal. Once the worm is removed, the chance of re-infection is high if the original security vulnerability has not been patched. Worms are pure cyber attack code in a single package and one of the worst vectors of possible cyber attack. If your computer is infected, it will seek out and infect as many computers as possible. Worms are cyber threat incarnate and history shows that they are getting more sophisticated and dangerous every year.

2002: The Melissa worm used a Microsoft Word macro-virus that accessed the Outlook address book and mailed itself to everybody on the list. Around 100,000 computers were compromised by the Melissa worm and the author was eventually tracked down and sent to jail for 20 months.

2002: The Nimda worm became the fastest growing internet worm in history as it exploited multiple vulnerabilities and backdoors left by other malware. Within 22 minutes of release, Nimda infected around 90 per cent of all possible vulnerable computers, estimated between 200,000 and 700,000 machines worldwide.

2003: Within ten minutes SQL Slammer infected over 75,000 computers across the planet, and caused massive collateral damage to the internet in the process. Each infected computer sent out huge streams of packets in an attempt to locate other vulnerable computers' servers,and routers and hubs crashed, causing a slowdown of traffic across the internet. Banking was rendered impossible for many people as over 13,000 ATM machines failed.

2004: The Sasser worm infected between 500,000 and one million computers worldwide. The German author was finally sentenced to probation and community service. It cannot be calculated how much time and energy was wasted cleaning up the global infection.

2004: The "MyDoom" worm harvested email addresses from between 300,000 and 500,000 infected computers. The use of email as the cyber attack vector meant that an estimated 25 per cent of all email sent across the internet at the time was generated by the MyDoom worm. Interestingly the MyDoom worm contains the text message "andy; I'm just doing my job, nothing personal, sorry," leading many to believe that the worm's creator was paid.

> **The Stuxnet worm... At the point of discovery it had infected over 100,000 computers, of which over 60 per cent were located in Iran.**

2008: The Conficker worm infected an estimated 15 million computers on the internet. The attack caused problems for the Ministry of Defence and Manchester's police. Some security experts believe that the Conficker worm is laying dormant in thousands of computers waiting to be activated at a later date.

2010: The Stuxnet worm is discovered in the wild by security researchers. At the point of discovery it had infected over 100,000 computers, of which over 60 per cent were located in Iran.

When security researchers analyzed Stuxnet, they found it to be a unique hybrid that targeted industrial control systems using Siemens Supervisory Control And Date Acquisitions (SCADA) systems. The Stuxnet worm would search for a specific software component on the target computer and then replace it with a copy. This allowed the worm to rewrite the Programmable Logic Chip (PLC) in the system to install rootkits and system monitoring trojans. The Stuxnet worm was capable of recording normal data flow patterns and then re-playing them to system operators to lull them into a false sense of security – much in the same way that the Zeus banking trojan sends false information to the victims of cyber-criminals whilst ransacking their bank accounts.

So what makes Stuxnet unique? For one thing, it is a monumental piece of software that was written by a team. It has been estimated that even with the modular design of Stuxnet it would have taken several people years to complete. Who would have designed and built such a worm? Was the Stuxnet worm the first ever cyber weapon to be used against SCADA infrastructure?

From analyzing the facts about the Stuxnet worm, it is obvious that:

- The majority of infected sites were in Iran – around 60 per cent – and another 30 per cent was spread across Asia. However, US sites sufferedonly a 0.6 per cent rate of infection, a fact that is surprising given the large number of Windows users in the USA.
- The Stuxnet worm contained attack components that only targeted Siemens SCADA systems. By replacing a critical system software component, Stuxnet had full control of communications and allowed manipulation of data-flow within the SCADA system, including monitoring and replay facilities. The Stuxnet worm had the capability of rewriting the PLC containing the control software and a rootkit to hide the modifications.
- The Stuxnet worm was written by a programming team of people with highly specialized knowledge of Siemens SCADA systems. The individual components bear the digital fingerprints – the coding style – of a group of people. The sophistication of the Stuxnet software means that one, or more, of the malware developers had a deep technical knowledge of Siemens SCADA systems.

If these simple facts are not enough to determine whether Stuxnet was a cyber weapon, the following information, at the very least, is highly suggestive.

During the Stuxnet attack, Iran allegedly suffered damage to approximately 1,000 centrifuges used for Uranium enrichment at the nuclear research establishment in Natanz. After many denials by Iranian officials, in November 2010, the president of Iran, Mahmoud Ahmadinejad, acknowledged that the Iranian nuclear program had been damaged by an unspecified malware infection, but insisted that Iranian software engineers had patched the vulnerability and that it was no longer exploitable. Ahmadinejad did not, however, mention the Stuxnet malware by name.

The final clue to the puzzle is deep inside the code itself and suggests that good old-fashioned espionage was used to discover the key frequencies used by the Iranian enrichment centrifuges. The Iranians are suspected of running their centrifuges at 1,007 cycles per second, a relatively low speed that is dictated by their crude IR–1 centrifuge based on designs provided by A.Q. Khan, the father of Pakistan's atomic bomb.

The Stuxnet worm did two things that were damaging to the Iranian centrifuges, Firstly, it would speed up the centrifuge to 1,064 cycles per second, then slow it down repeatedly. Secondly, the rootkit inside the Programmable Logic Controller (PLC) and the customized communications DLL (Dynamic Link Library), which was a component of the Windows operating system, allowed for the recording of all the sensor parameters being monitored by the SCADA system. This stream of system data could then be replayed at will, while the centrifuges were sent out of control, and this false data would prevent the operators from realizing that anything was wrong and shutting down the system. It seems that the Stuxnet parameters were precisely calibrated to send the Iranian centrifuges out of control.

A final hint that this was an attack targeted at the Iranian uranium enrichment program is that code in Stuxnet appears to be searching for 984 machines linked together. When the Natanz uranium enrichment plant was visited by International Atomic Energy Agency (IAEA) inspectors in 2011, they found that exactly 984 centrifuges were no longer working and later reported than Iran had temporarily suspended work on uranium enrichment.

So, it appears that the Stuxnet worm was designed to do one thing and one thing only: to attack and destroy as many of the Iranian uranium enrichment centrifuges as possible, thereby directly slowing down the progress of the Iranian nuclear program. From this we can conclude that this was not malware designed as a banking theft trojan (such as the Zeus bot), nor is it the run-of-the-mill black-hat malware bot designed for DDoS attacks, credential theft or adware installation. All the evidence points to the fact that Stuxnet was a sophisticated cyber weapon designed by nation-state actors as a tool of cyberwar.

But which nation state was responsible for the design and development of Stuxnet? Initial speculation led to the conclusion that at least two countries were involved in the development of Stuxnet – Israel and the USA. That said, France and the UK also have the capabilities.

Evidence unearthed by *The New York Times (NYT)* suggests that, as early as 2008, the Department of Homeland Security teamed up with Siemens researchers[17] to test for vulnerabilities in Siemens' SIMATIC PCS 7. The intelligence community already knew that the Iranians' were using these systems to control their uranium enrichment centrifuges, and in 2009, the USA successfully lobbied the United Arab Emirates to block a shipment of 111 SIMATIC S7 systems from Dubai into Iran. Researchers have concluded that at least one of the programmers of the Stuxnet worm was a specialist in Siemens' SIMATIC S7 systems. Did Siemens loan a programmer to the project or was it a programmer gone rogue?

Stuxnet was a dedicated "one shot" weapon with a single target and indicates the nature of future cyber-weaponry.

The stated objective of the database modification attack was to infiltrate the PCS 7 and modify the configuration of the system without being detected, as Siemens' themselves state in their presentation given at the 2008 Automation Summit, "a hacker modifying a controller configuration would be a significant security breach." Strangely enough, this is exactly the same method that the Stuxnet worm used to penetrate and reconfigure the database and install a rootkit on the actual PLC controller itself. Did the Department of Homeland Security and Siemens share the results with

---

17 "Control Systems Security Assessments", Marty Edwards (Idaho National Laboratory) and Todd Staufer (Siemens), *Automation Summit: A Users Conference*, Chicago, 2008

the writers or the Stuxnet worm? Or were they more heavily involved?

The *NYT* investigation has gone further, quoting anonymous sources to suggest that the Stuxnet worm was tested in the months prior to the attack both in the USA, in Israel and possibly in England. If these allegations are true, then it seems likely that the Stuxnet worm was a joint project between the USA, the UK and Israel designed with the express purpose of derailing the Iranian nuclear project.

Was Stuxnet a success? As a cyber weapon it was designed to be fired like a digital arrow, to hit a single target, and slowly and steadily infect over 100,000 computers. At each step of the way it would ask the following questions: (a) is this computer running in a SCADA environment? (b) is the SCADA environment Siemens? (c) is it a Siemens System 7? and (d) is it attached to the right kind of electrical motor? As one cyber-security expert pointed out, "unless you were running uranium nuclear enrichment centrifuges, it wasn't going to hurt you." Stuxnet kept digital collateral damage to a minimum – and had it not been discovered by accident, the kill switch date would have deleted the software from the infected computers. Stuxnet was the perfect digital stealth weapon.

In that sense Stuxnet was a success. The success can be measured in the two years lost by the Iranian uranium nuclear enrichment effort. The success can be measured in the fact that it was a highly effective, low-cost cyber weapon with high levels of plausible deniability. Stuxnet was a dedicated one shot weapon with a single target and indicates the nature of future cyber weaponry. The use of cyber weapons and covert digital warfare is a powerful force multiplier for any country. Although the USA has never formally admitted responsibility for the development and release of the Stuxnet worm, in 2013 the NSA whistle blower Edward Snowden confirmed the 2011 report in the *New York Times*.

The *New York Times* has alleged that the development of Stuxnet was part of a cyber warfare effort called Operation Olympic Games, which was started by George W. Bush and continued under Barack Obama. Recently it has been alleged that the source of the leaks to *The New York Times* is retired US General James Cartwright who is thought to be under investigation by the US Justice Department. Currently, there is no strong evidence that the USA was involved in the development of the Stuxnet malware but the circumstantial evidence presented in the media strongly suggests the involvement of the world's largest cyber-power.[18]

Stuxnet – and other alleged cyber weapons such as Flame or Duqu – are the precursor to a new world of digital risk. Stuxnet might have escaped into the wild by mistake, but once isolated it became like any other piece of computer code – infinitely replicable. The idea of Stuxnet is a virus in itself. Once the idea of a weaponized piece of malware such as the Stuxnet worm is unleashed into the public consciousness, every country will want one.

Now anybody can download the Stuxnet source code from the internet. Anybody can learn from the computing code and the techniques used by Stuxnet. The Stuxnet code makes the world a less safe place and allows the development of a whole new generation of cyber weapons designed to attack critical infrastructure by subverting the SCADA systems that control that infrastructure. The use of Stuxnet as a cyber weapon has opened a Pandora's Box of new cyber threats, leading to the new digital arms race as the domain of cyberspace becomes inevitably militarized.

18 http://abcnews.go.com/blogs/headlines/2013/07/edward-snowden-u-s-israel-co-wrote-cyber-super-weapon-stuxnet/

13

CYBER ATTACK

The increasing militarization of cyberspace has led to the development of a whole new vector of cyber attack. The development of cyber weapons such as Stuxnet, Flame and Duqu is leading to a new cyber arms race. The most dangerous emerging threat from new types of cyber weapons are the weapons that target the essential infrastructure of a country. When cyber weapons of this nature are unleashed, the potential for both physical and digital collateral damage is enormous.

The new types of cyber weapons take covert digital warfare into the next generation. These weapons do not just affect the infrastructure of the internet itself, they project from the digital cyberworld into the real world with horrifying effects. How can infrastructure attacks across cyberspace be so important and dangerous? Because the targets for cyber attacks are the programming codes and the data that run the computer systems which rule our lives. Attacking any one of them could cause chaos. Attacking one or more could cripple the economy and cause hundreds of thousands of real, not virtual, mortalities.

What is SCADA? Why is it important? SCADA – Supervisory Control and Data Acquisition – is basically just software. SCADA is the software that runs large industrial plants and more. The software that runs our civilisation and thus SCADA is an important part of our lives. Most people think of software as something than runs on our computers, laptops, tablets and smartphones. The dark truth is that software is everywhere and in everything – your washing machine, your fridge, your microwave and your car. Software is the most common invention of the modern industrial age, changing everything just as surely as the invention of the steam engine changed everything. Software has invaded our lives, but the invisible software that controls modern infrastructure is even more important. We can't see it – but it is there and it is under cyber attack on a daily basis.

Our modern civilization relies on the industrial processes that fuel our world. Power plants, sewage treatment plants, water pumping stations and our gas and oil pipelines are maintained and monitored using computer-based SCADA systems, and many can be controlled online. It is estimated that after the release of the Stuxnet worm there were 20 times more vulnerabilities discovered in SCADA systems than in the previous ten years.

The current list of targets for SCADA cyber attacks reads like the list from a science fiction movie. Any of these cyber attacks – or a combination – can bring a country to a halt in an instant. When 94 per cent of all information stored in the world is digital, a combination of cyber attacks across the planet could bring on the tipping point that destroys our civilization.

The problem is that SCADA vulnerabilities are *everywhere*. So what types of infrastructure attacks could ruin our society?

Communications

Attacking the telephone infrastructure would make life impossible. Even the internet, designed to be resilient enough to survive a nuclear attack, runs on the phone lines. Destroying the communications infrastructure degrades any country's ability to respond to a crisis. Combined with other attacks on this list, it amplifies and acts as a force multiplier for those cyber attacks. Strangely enough, communications would be the last thing to be attacked, as it is the primary pathway of assault for most cyber attacks. Nor would satellite phones be safe. There has been several reports of satellites being compromised by hackers. An attack on GPS satellites would not necessarily destroy the GPS system. It is far more effective to feed false data to personnel using GPS, causing massive confusion and disruption.

Finance

Attacking the financial infrastructure of an enemy country is not just the idea of coordinated attacks on the stock market or automated trading systems. An infrastructure attack on a country could be limited to denying the target population access to their money from ATMs and automated banking systems. This would degrade the possibility of purchasing essential goods, queues would form and the possibility of panic, hoarding and looting would become real. Cyber attacks on the financial systems are easy; even ordinary malware such as worms can knock out networks of ATMs and have the effect of lowering the morale of ordinary citizens in the target nation.

Transportation

The automated computer systems that monitor and control our transportation networks are everywhere. Computer programs run traffic control systems. Imagine the chaos if every traffic light in a city turned red and stayed there. Worse yet, imagine if they all went green. Computer systems run our rapid transit systems. Newer systems such as East London's Docklands Light Railway are entirely controlled by computers. The SCADA systems of inner city subway systems are often old. Intervention in any of those systems would bring subways to a halt or worse. Large motorways often have information systems that alert the driver of problems such as fog, freezing conditions, delays and pile-ups. Imagine the chaos that would ensue if a covert cyber weapon temporarily suspended all operations. All cyber attacks on transportation infrastructure have a side effect: they tie up all of the first responders, the ambulance service, police and fire fighters required to sort out the mess – and this just adds to the cyber-chaos.

Energy

There are SCADA systems in almost every electricity substation and gas distribution platform available. This allows the central HQ to monitor and control the amount of flow, redistribute loads and ensure that citizens do not freeze to death in the winter. Attacking both types of energy plant would plunge a city into a cold darkness. Nothing would work. Our civilization is so dependent on electricity and gas that we only notice its absence. But there is a huge physical collateral damage in this type of attack. People would be trapped in lifts, in the subway and in other forms of transport that rely on electricity, such as trams and "smart trains".

Water and Sewage

The SCADA water and sewage systems in large cities are often interlinked. Both deal with a similar issue: providing water to the population, draining excess water and draining and treating sewage. These highly sophisticated systems are vulnerable. By attacking water pump substations attached to the central controller, access to water can be denied to an entire city population. If you attack systems used to control water run-off, through a network of pipes and pumping stations, an entire area can be flooded very easily. If you attack the sewage filtration system, sewage that would normally be treated could be release into a river, causing massive ecological collateral damage that would take years to heal. Worse yet is the "Dam Busters" cyber attack. Instead of using a bomb, an aggressor could use a SCADA cyber weapon that releases all the water behind a dam used for generating hydro-electric power. The result of the attack would be not only the inundation of villages, fields and towns by water flowing downstream but also a direct degradation of enemy performance on electricity generation.

Oil Refineries

An oil refinery is a huge machine. Over many years the evolution of oil refineries has made them more efficient and easier to manage. This is due to the advanced SCADA systems that monitor and allow operators to maintain capacity and be alerted to problems that could threaten production or even the refinery itself. Advanced cyber weapons such as variations of Stuxnet could take control of vital valves and control processes inside the refinery. The consequences would be unthinkable. Just shutting a valve while reporting it was open could lead to a huge build-up of pressure while shutting many key valves would lead to an explosion. Oil refineries are a dangerous installation at the best of times, but a properly planned cyber attack on an oil refinery would degrade the production of petro-chemicals for a long time. Attack them all at once and billions of dollars would literally go up in smoke.

Nuclear Power

A nuclear power station needs to be controlled, and that control is passed to the operators in the control room who use an advanced SCADA system. In a nuclear power plant, nothing should go wrong because there are often systems with multiple redundancies to prevent failure. These does not always work, as proved by the Chernobyl and Fukushima nuclear disasters of 1986 and 2011 respectively. A successful cyber attack on a nuclear power plant is the ultimate cyber weapon. If the plant were merely disabled, the cyber attack would have ceased the ability of the enemy to produce electricity. If the plant were partially destroyed, then the possibility of radiation leak would tie up resources in a clean up operation. If a nuclear meltdown were to be induced by raising the damping rods while falsifying the data readouts to the operators, for example, then the impact would be severe. The evacuation of the local population, the necessity for screening for radiation poisoning and the provision of enough food and water for a refugee population that could be in the hundreds of thousands would be a huge strain on the resources for the country attacked.

This all sounds like scary stuff. Surely the current cyberwar hype is just the Military Industrial Complex trying to scare us into allowing it to have a larger budget? Alas not; there is strong evidence to suggest that this digital covert war has been playing out for a number of years, even predating the Stuxnet attack on Iranian uranium enrichment facilities.

How vulnerable are we to SCADA-based infrastructure attacks? There have been a number of SCADA incidents over the years. Listed below are just a few. Nobody knows if these were just a software failure in the SCADA systems or cyber attacks that deployed cyber weapons. The essence of the covert cyberwar is plausible deniability or digital *maskirovka*.

But the history of alleged cyber attacks shows a distinct evolutionary process – cyber attacks are getting worse every year.

- 1982. Siberian pipeline explosion– an alleged trojan was inserted into SCADA software
- 1992. Chevron – a former employee disabled the emergency system in 22 US states
- 1994. Roosevelt Dam – a hacker breaks into floodgate SCADA systems
- 1997. A NYNEX hack cuts of all communications to Worcester Airport in Massachusetts, USA
- 1999. Bellingham, Washington – a gasoline pipeline failure
- 2000. Sewage dump – disaffected Australian sewage worker employee dumps one million gallons of raw sewage into the environment
- 2000. Gazprom – hackers gain control of Russian natural gas pipeline
- 2003. Slammer worm cripples airlines and affects 130 ATMs
- 2003. The Sobig virus cripples the CSX Train Signaling System
- 2005.The Zotob worms attacks car factories
- 2007. California canal system SCADA.hack
- 2008. Hatch Nuclear Power Plant shutdown
- 2009. US hospital SCADA systems attacked by employee
- 2010. Stuxnet attacks uranium enrichment program, Iran
- 2011. Russian hackers destroy water pump in Illinois, USA
- 2011. Hacker demonstrates SCADA vulnerability in Houston, USA
- 2012. Virus infects 55,000 computers of the Saudi Arabian Oil Co, Saudi Arabia

The history of SCADA cyber attacks indicates that cyberwar has become a reality. Cyberspace is becoming a battlefield and the primary targets are the SCADA systems that our society depends on. Cyberspace is becoming militarized without us being aware of it and the consequences are potentially lethal.

A recent report[19] underlined the common misconceptions about SCADA systems:

1. **SCADA systems reside on a physically separate, stand-alone network.** This assumption is incorrect. As the internet has grown there are more and more interconnections between the "back office" computers and the SCADA network. Even a laptop or a memory stick connected to the SCADA system could create system vulnerability. This was the possible vector for the cyber attack of the Stuxnet worm.

2. **SCADA controls and other corporate systems are protected by "strong access controls".** If the SCADA system is connected to the corporate network, then the protection of the SCADA system is only as strong as the weakest link in the network. The use of remote desktop access with default passwords, network shares and other features of modern computer life are all vectors of attack on the SCADA systems. Compromise of any part of the corporate network could allow compromise of the SCADA systems.

3. **SCADA systems require specialized knowledge, making them difficult for network intruders to access and control.** The makers and developers of SCADA systems publish system specifications for their SCADA products; they develop toolkits to assist software developers to write code for the SCADA systems; and the standards used by interoperating SCADA systems are well documented and well distributed. There is no "security by obscurity" option for SCADA networks – too many people are involved in designing, building and writing software for them.

How widespread are SCADA vulnerabilities? Between 2011 and 2012 over 50 new SCADA exploits were published, whereas in the year before a mere six were published. A recent study suggested that only 42 per cent of all SCADA systems are fully secure and that 17 per cent are vulnerable to known exploits. This leaves a large number of SCADA systems – 41 per cent – that are possibly vulnerable to new exploits. Like always, laziness on the part of system's administrators' account for nearly a third of all system vulnerabilities. Default passwords kill system security. The SCADA

19 RIPTECH, "Understanding SCADA system security vulnerabilities" 2001

attack surface is huge and widely distributed across the world. It is estimated that over 31 per cent of the total number SCADA systems available via the internet are in the USA while over 41 per cent are in Europe. Given the Chinese cyberwar posture, it should be no surprise to find that China has the lowest number of internet-attached SCADA systems – a mere 1.1 per cent of the total.

The patch problem within SCADA systems is as bad as it is in other computer systems. It is estimated that only 81 per cent of all system vulnerabilities are fixed in a timely manner; the other 19 per cent takes up to 30 days before the system is patched. This is a window of opportunity – a properly applied zero day exploit could lead to rootkit insertion of malware that can persist even after the security hole is fixed. What is even worse, is that many systems are so old they are never upgraded – those risks will endure forever.

A honeypot is a computer that has been set up to attract hackers and cyber-criminals. It monitors everything and gathers information about hacking methods.

The danger of possible SCADA attacks was demonstrated recently by research using internet honeypots. A honeypot is a computer that has been set up to attract hackers and cyber-criminals. It monitors everything, enabling security researchers to gather valuable information about modern methods of cyber warfare and even harvest malware such as worms and RATs as they are installed across the internet. In this instance a security researcher placed three different SCADA honeypots on the internet – each of which looked exactly like a genuine SCADA system and contained what appeared to be genuine SCADA software security risks. Within 18 hours the honeypots were under attack and over 28 days there were 39 attacks from 14 different countries. Looking at the location of the attackers determined that 35 per cent appeared to originate from China but that 19 per cent appeared to originate from the USA. Of course, determining the true originator of the cyber attacks is difficult. A hacker from the USA could exploit a hacked server in China. Perhaps this explains why 12 per cent of the attacks appeared to originate from Laos – not exactly known for its cyber warfare capabilities; Chinese and US hackers may have bounced off servers in Laos itself.

The release of Stuxnet into the world has focused attention on the risks inside SCADA software. Now anyone who wants to test for SCADA security failures can buy pre-packaged attack software. The recently announced Agora SCADA+ package includes nine zero day exploits inside a package designed to probe SCADA controllers. For just a handful of bucks you can buy the software that can bring a country to its knees. Malware is the AK–47 of the digital revolutionary.

The current problem facing the world with regard to cyber attacks on SCADA systems is a fluke of history. When the original systems were designed they often used closed serial networks with proprietary network protocols that allowed only trusted devices to connect. The rapid growth of the internet has led to the connection of more and more devices running the TCP/IP protocol, each of which is potentially insecure. When the SCADA protocols were designed, nobody thought about security – the systems used leased lines and very expensive modems. Now that we live in an age of interconnectivity – undreamt of by the designers of these systems – we are all living with cyber threats. The release of Stuxnet has unlocked Pandora's Box and the world is now a more dangerous place. The militarization of cyberspace is advancing rapidly and the internet itself has become a weapon. The release of Stuxnet has unlocked Pandora's Box and the modern world is more dangerous place.

SECTION 3

CYBER-PARANOIA

"I don't want to live in a world where there's no privacy, and therefore no room for intellectual exploration and creativity."

Edward Snowden, NSA whistleblower

Cyber-technology has allowed the world to communicate and exchange ideas more than ever before in history. The majority of us email, post and surf the internet on a daily basis and although our actions may be innocent, there are others who use cyberspace with darker intentions. This raises the question of whether cyber activity should be monitored. If so, to what degree? And how should this information be managed?

14

DIGITAL PANOPTICON

Users of the internet live in a digital goldfish bowl where every movement is watched by anyone who is interested. Our adoption of social networking websites means that we share more information about our lives than ever before. We have become preoccupied with our own internet presence. We update our weblogs and statuses and we tweet about the most inane of things. We live in the age of what some pundits have called the digital panopticon.

The original idea of the panopticon was conceived by the philosopher Jeremy Bentham in 1786. It was designed as an ideal prison where every inmate could be watched at any time by any of the guards – but nobody knew when they were being watched. The philosophy behind the panopticon was simple: if nobody knew if they were being watched at any time, they would assume they were being watched all the time. In a sense, the prisoners themselves became the guards as they automatically behave as if they were being watched.

For some social scientists the internet is a treasure trove of data just waiting to be tapped into. As Duncan J. Watts, the author of *Everything Is Obvious Once You Know The Answer,* writes:

Imagine if all the data from Facebook, Google, Yahoo!, Foursquare, Twitter, and GroupOn were combined. Now imagine if all that data were combined with all the location data, call and SMS records for all cellular phones. In fact, imagine that everyone had smartphones, and that all the app usage data were also combined.

Then imagine combining all that data with data from shoppers club cards, retailer databases, credit agencies, voter registration records, presidential campaign contributions, real estate transactions, credit card transactions.

Watts suggests that combining all this data would allow social scientists to learn about human social interactions and behavior that is considered mysterious, by collecting and analyzing this data for very large groups of people for an extended period of time. He adds that "viewed this way, the digital panopticon might revolutionize social science the way that the telescope revolutionized physics".[20]

Duncan Watts, a principal research scientist at Yahoo!, is looking on the bright side of life. We are already living in a global digital panopticon. We are already watched, profiled, filed and archived. Almost everything we do in our lives is archived on a computer somewhere in cyberspace. But cyberspace is inherently flexible. Data and code intermingle in open and dangerous ways and the data that defines our lives is often in the hands of corporations that care little for modern ideas of privacy and security. The same conveniences that define our lives in the twenty-first century are also threats in themselves. When added to the convenience of the internet, these threats multiply and become cyber threats.

CCTV

Closed circuit television cameras have been around for years – but the explosion in Wi-Fi and bluetooth enabled cameras make them easier to install due to the lack of cables. There are an estimated 4–5.9 million CCTV cameras in the UK alone, according to a 2013 report from the British Security Industry Association (BSIA). In the US, the number of surveillance cameras is thought to be in excess of 10 million. While there are checks and balances on government-owned CCTV footage, private companies own their footage and it routinely turns up on the internet. The increasing use of digital technology for CCTV cameras means that computerized backup systems make it easier and cheaper to keep footage for longer and longer.

20 *Scientific American* April 25, 2011

Cell phones

In 2013 there were an estimated six billion cell phones in the world and this is expected to rise to nearly 7.3 billion by 2014[21]. Countries with poor telephonic infrastructure using traditional cables have skipped a generation of technology and uptake has been faster. For example, in Russia there are between 1.5 and 1.8 times as many cell phones as there are people.

But every cell phone is a tracking device. The techniques used by cell phones to communicate with the local tower enable easy surveillance. As you move from cell to cell, it is possible to triangulate the cell phone signal and predict the movement of a suspect. Your cell phone is like an electronic handcuff that allows the tracking of your every move. Your calls are logged – time, date, place, number called and duration – possibly even more. Your voicemail is recorded on a server somewhere and the data could possibly be stored for years if the phone company is keeping long-term digital backups. GPS-enabled phones allow for surveillance with more accuracy than normal cell-phones. The GPS features on your smartphone stores meta-data such as time and location inside the files containing any pictures taken with that phone, even if you turn the GPS tracking features off. Several telecommunications companies are experimenting with local triangulation to record movements of shoppers inside large stores and shopping malls.

Credit Cards

The ease and convenience of credit cards has seen an explosion in their usage over the last 30 years. There are now an estimated five billion credit cards in the world, which would be almost one for every person on the planet, except that 1.5 billion are in the USA[22]. Every time a credit card transaction is made, it is verified in real time across the phone system or internet. Every credit card is a tracking device but not quite as efficient as a cell phone because it helps to locate a suspect only when used. What credit cards can is to allow data-mining by advertisers and marketing people to more efficiently target consumers with certain patterns of

21 Source: http://www.digitaltrends.com/mobile/mobile-phone-world-population-2014/
22 Source http://www.statisticbrain.com/credit-card-ownership-statistics/

behavior – men who buy beer and nappies on a Friday night, for example. The downside is that your purchasing behavior is tracked, logged and filed for future use and may even be sold on to other agencies.

Travel Cards

If a credit card is convenient, the convenience of a travel card is even greater. For frequent passengers on public transport, the time saved with a travel card is priceless – but there is a downside. Every journey you make using that card is logged somewhere and your precise movements can be tracked through the use of your card. The Oyster card in London is a good example of this. Even though the operating agency denies keeping data beyond a few months or so, it might still be lurking somewhere on the monthly backups. In the cyber-age, data is hardly ever fully erased as professional business information technologists design backup schemes that keep data for between three and five years. I recently asked for details on my travel card and was provided with a huge roll of paper that tracked the dates, times and journeys taken for the last four years.

Internet Usage

Internet tracking is the brave new world of consumer science. The only reason why Google and Facebook can make money is by tracking your behaviour and targeting you with advertisements that are – allegedly – tailored to your needs. These internet companies are not in the business of facilitating communication; they are sucking up huge amounts of raw data about consumer preferences. Google probably knows more about your likes and dislikes than your best friend – it matches your profile to other profiles and serves up what it *thinks* you need. We live in an age when the machines know us better than perhaps we know ourselves.

Cyber-censorship

As large search engines such as Google and Yahoo! build censorware versions of their websites across China, and as more countries seek to restrict the free flow of information across the internet, the cyber-curtains are coming down across the world as we approach the limits of free speech on the internet. The increasing use of blacklist censorware means that companies can use their power to censor sites critical of their activities. Libraries and educational institutions use censorware that blocks inappropriate material and which denies legitimate researchers access to a range of websites. Meanwhile, the UK has been trying to force ISPs to install censorware that not only fails to prevent access to illegal material, but can actually be reverse-engineered to provide a directory of websites that host illegal material.

Satellite Surveillance

With the advent of Google Earth, anyone can find ground images of anything on the planet. But how much better are the military satellites than the commercial satellites used by Google? With recent technological breakthroughs the commercial satellite companies will be able to offer satellite imagery at one-quarter meter per pixel resolution – something only previously used for military and intelligence gathering purposes – to anyone who can pay. It is currently estimated that the market for satellite-based imagery used for business intelligence and other purposes will grow to be at least $4 billion (£2.5 billion) a year by 2018. The uses of this data is limited only by the imagination of the purchasers.

All this would be fine. After all, who doesn't want our consumer experience to be faster and better? Who doesn't want to protect children from inappropriate material on the internet? Avoiding unwanted advertisements should be a boon to mankind because highly targeted advertising should make our lives easier and more efficient. The mass of information collected by internet companies should be a benefit – and not a cyber threat – to the users of the internet.

None of this would be important if the internet was colonized only by advertising and marketing executives. Even if the "fifth domain" is only used to track purchases and internet behavior for the sole purpose of selling something to somebody, somewhere in the world the data involving the lives of innocent people is up for sale. The digital panopticon should be the major beneficial change to emerge from the coming cyber-age, but the digital panopticon has a dark side.

The internet was still growing when everything changed. Suddenly a new force emerged as a coordinated wave of terrorist attacks across the globe shattered the post Cold War optimism. The ultimate terrorist spectacle was the attack on the World Trade Center and the destruction of the twin towers on September 11, 2001. These events were watched live and beamed around the world – an act of terrorism that promoted the message of militant Jihadi beliefs across the world.

Automated computerized surveillance systems have grown in size and sophistication, sucking up vast amounts of data from multiple systems and then correlating it.

The US response was to announce long-term plans to battle global Islamist Terrorism, which was defined as a "conflict fought in dozens of countries and for decades to come." According to the statements made by President Bush the Western bloc needed to fight "a generation-long war against Islamic radicalism". Suddenly the search for the "enemy within" that had ended with the collapse of communism had returned – but now the enemy were Islamic terrorists rather than "reds under the bed". Intelligence programs are designed to routinely monitor citizens as the search for "the enemy within" intensifies. Automated computerized surveillance systems have grown in size and sophistication, sucking up vast amounts of data from multiple systems and then correlating it. The current volume of data contained by the computer systems dedicated to fighting the war on terror make the legendary German Stasi archives look tiny by comparison.

Digital counter insurgency will be fought in information space. The weapons are powerful computers that collect, store and correlate vast amounts of data – and the target is you.

In the war against Communism, the citizens were not watched continuously by CCTV cameras that connected to computers which could match number plates and faces, and their financial transactions were not routinely data-mined for patterns that fitted the profile of terrorists, drugs dealers or money launderers. Their movements were not tracked by RFID smart-cards embedded into travel cards and old phone technology would never have allowed for every phone call to be logged – let alone monitored. There were no cell phones allowing geo-tracking using GPS and the internet – itself an outgrowth of the war on Communism – had yet to make the impact it has in the modern world.

Here we have arrived at the true heart of darkness of the idea of the digital panopticon: a network of global surveillance that is more ubiquitous than anything imagined by George Orwell in *1984*. In the age of information warfare, computers will track, list, watch, compile and cross-compile files on anyone who is considered a suspect – and in the new digital age *everybody* is a suspect, including you.

For this reason the growth of ubiquitous, systematic surveillance by computer systems is one of the biggest threats democracies currently face: Who programs these systems? Are they confidential? Who has access to them? What will happen when the data is incorrect or the programmer makes a mistake? How reliable and accurate are these systems?

15

THE "FAKE" INTERNET

One of the criticisms leveled against the information on the worldwide web is the lack of quality control. How reliable is the information on the internet? The debate normally centers around the neutrality – or lack of neutrality – of the information provided by certain websites such as Wikipedia and Encyclopedia Britannica. But there is another side to the debate: How many internet users are genuine people? How many websites are really what they seem?

The phenomena of the fake internet is growing on a daily basis and threatens to undermine user confidence in the reality of the internet. Here are the most common identifiers of the fake internet – a digital shadow-world where nothing is what it seems.

Sock Puppets

Sock puppets are false internet users designed to mislead or deceive genuine users by pretending to be somebody they're not. Websites that provide forums, or weblogs, that allow comments, will often ban users who are destructive to an online community – trolls – but once banned the user can easily come back with another identity. Sock puppets are also employed by companies involved in **astro turfing** and by cyber-criminals, but the majority of sock puppets are false online identities used by individuals. For example, the social networking site Digg allows for the posting, sharing and rating of internet links by the use of crowdsourcing techniques to highlight the relative importance of content on the web. By using multiple sock puppets, an individual can post material that appears to come from a neutral source – i.e. an article on a weblog or a particular website. When multiple sock puppets then rate the posted article with a positive rating, it generates traffic to the website. More traffic and more views means a higher chance of somebody clicking through on a web advertisement – generating more income for the website owner. The use of Digg in this way can be so effective that websites become unavailable due to overloading or lead to very high hosting bills for the website owners. This has actually become known as the Digg Effect due to the large number of websites that have suffered in this way.

Another use of sock puppets is by cyber-criminals who are using social networking sites to support their criminal activities. Social networking sites are useful for cyber-criminals searching for new victims for their scams. Due to the way social networking sites work – based effectively on a circle of trust – users are more likely to include somebody as a friend of a friend than a total stranger. By exploiting multiple sock puppet identities, cyber-criminals can access a vast pool of potential victims. Nobody knows the full extent of the problem, but the size of the threat can be estimated from the activities of the cyber-criminal KoobFace gang. At the height of their cybercrime spree, the KoobFace gang had an estimated 50,000 fake Google based Gmail and Blogger accounts, and more than 20,000 fake Facebook accounts. Other cyber-gangs could be running even more sock puppets as the software designed to run multiple online identities – persona management software – becomes available on the criminal black market. The Koobface gang made their money from pay-per install of fake anti-virus software, adware and click-redirection software that facilitated click fraud. Although each paid installation earned only a few cents or dollars, it has been estimated that the Koobface gang earned over $2 million dollars per year.

Finally, it should be pointed out that even security experts can be fooled by sock puppets. Thomas Ryan, a computer security expert for Provide Security LLC, conducted an experiment in 2010, when he created a sock puppet that purported to be a computer security expert.[23] This sock puppet identified herself "Robin Sage" and claimed to work as a Cyber Threat Analyst for the Naval Network Warfare Command, suggesting that she had security clearance from the US government. By targeting known security experts, the fictitious security expert was able to penetrate the circle of trust surrounding cyber-security experts. The snowball effect inherent in social networking meant that by friending known security experts, "Robin Sage" gained almost instant acceptance inside the cyber security community. Over a 28-day period "Robin Sage" accumulated hundreds of connections across a number of social networking sites, including contacts at NSA, Department of Defense, NASA and a number of large corporations. Strangely enough, only a handful of people did their homework and concluded that the "Robin Sage" was a sock puppet. The "Robin Sage" experiment showed just how easy it was to spread a false persona across the internet. If cyber-security experts can be fooled, what chance do members of the general public have?

Astro Turfing

Astro turfing is the use of sock puppets by corporations in an attempt to influence public opinion on the internet. The phrase is derived from the brand of synthetic grass called AstroTurf, which is often used in sports arenas. The use of sock puppets makes it appear that the grassroots share a belief or set of beliefs that support the agenda of the organization using the fake internet identities. This allows false information to be injected into the internet while masking the true source of the disinformation, which can be useful in attempts at viral marketing. It could be the case that a single user is pretending to be dozens of people across many different forums or websites, and companies now hire internet users to lurk for months or even years across the web, until the time is right for all users to promote the same message.

In 2013 Wikipedia began an investigation of the use of sock puppets used to write articles promoting companies and products while not

23 Thomas, Ryan, "Getting into bed with Robin Sage"

disclosing their true identities or conflicts of interest. Sue Gardner, Wikimedia Foundation Executive Director, issued a statement explaining why Wikipedia had blocked over 250 user accounts: "unlike a university professor editing Wikipedia articles in their area of expertise, paid editing for promotional purposes, or paid advocacy editing as we call it, is extremely problematic. We consider it a 'black hat' practice." Wikipedia takes the problem of sock puppets and astro-turfing seriously, but the problem is growing.

Typically this kind of fake user will sign on to a website or weblog comments page and establish a level of trust with other readers of that page by bland but sensible comments. Establishing trust is important; other users are less likely to pay attention to known trolls or users who start flame wars than to users who seem entirely sensible. Once a reasonable level of trust is established, the fake users can then act spreading disinformation, propaganda or advertising messages while appearing to be from a neutral source.

There is software that exists that allows a single internet user to manage multiple fake identities across multiple websites and it has been estimated that over one third of all alleged consumer reviews on the internet are actually false. Some of these reviews promote products while others are critical of competing products, but the effect is to distort internet debate and insert false information onto the World Wide Web. In 2010 the US military acquired sophisticated software for the management of fake users, who are then used to spread messages which are supportive of US foreign policy and which can cause disruption of extremist groups and spreading propaganda. Although this software is not designed to be used in the USA due to legal restrictions, other computer security companies are also designing persona management software allowing a single user to control a huge number of sock puppets – which could be sold to anyone.

Infiltrators

We have seen the use of fake internet identities by cyber-criminals and corporations, but the use of false online identities by the government and military is a growing phenomenon. The first type of infiltrator would be the type of fake identity used by law enforcement agencies for both evidence collecting and crime prevention.

An example of this is the creation of the online identity Master Splyntr by the FBI agent J. Keith Mularski.[24] Using this fake persona, he was able to register with a large number of cybercrime forums and observe first hand what the cyber-criminals were doing. By setting up a false reputation as a Polish spam and phishing criminal, Mularski was able to gain the trust of several cyber-criminals. Once accepted inside their circle of trust, Mularski would then be accepted by other cyber-criminal forums, gaining more credibility with every new connection. Once Master Splyntr was established as a known cyber-criminal, Mularski was able to convince the administrator of the crime forum Dark Market to allow the website to be hosted on a secure server. In reality the server was provided by the FBI and Mularski had full access to everything that occurred in the forum. This provided valuable intelligence that later led to the arrest of Max Vision the systems administrator of the notorious cybercrime forum Carders Market. During the entire infiltration operation, the FBI was passing back information about stolen credit card details to banks and credit card companies, preventing further future cybercrime. Two years later, at the end of the operation, law enforcement agencies had made 56 arrests in four countries – a major blow for cyber-criminals everywhere.

> **Once accepted inside their circle of trust, Mularski would then be accepted by other cyber-criminal forums, gaining more credibility with every new connection.**

The second type of infiltrator is used by anti-terrorist experts, intelligence operatives and the military. As we have already seen there are a large number of websites on the internet hosting pro-militant jihadi material including videos of attacks on US troops, propaganda and instructional material. They are also very dangerous to monitor; the people who work in this field have to take extreme precautions to mask their true identities and locations as Al Qaeda would be ruthless if they

24 Kevin Poulson, *Kingpin: How One Hacker Took Over the Billion Dollar Cybercrime Underground*

caught them – and probably video their execution to post on the internet. Unlike the activities of the known hacktivist The Jester, who performs attacks on pro-jihadi websites using denial of service tools, the experts in infiltrating these forums keep a low profile. Once established inside the circle of trust of the terrorists, they can pose as fellow travellers and gather valuable intelligence about the terrorists.

Sting Boards

A sting board is a fake website set up on the internet by law enforcement or security agencies to monitor and trap criminal activity on the internet. The easiest sting boards were old school bulletin board systems (BBS), which were accessed using a modem. Law enforcement officials soon realized that a cost effective method of monitoring hacker activity was to set up a fake BBS which purported to be a forum for the exchange of hacking information and software. Modern sting boards are used for a variety of purposes:

- **Fighting child pornography:** The sting board purports to be a source of child pornography. While never showing the criminal any child pornography, the sting board will record the IP address of the abuser. Some sting boards even request details such as name and credit card details for billing purposes. Once the evidence has been obtained, this gives probable cause for a search warrant. The majority of criminals using child pornography are serial abusers and their computers can contain thousands of images of abuse – more than enough evidence to send them to jail for a long time.
- **Fighting cybercrime:** The undercover FBI agent Master Splyntr was successful in persuading cyber-criminals to host their pre-existing cybercrime website on a computer under FBI control, but this was a website that already existed. The use of sting boards has proved to be highly effective against credit card fraud and the recent Operation Card Shop provided enough evidence to arrest 24 people in 13 different countries. The FBI also regularly set up sting boards across the internet to fight a variety of cybercrime, such as the selling of illegal narcotics or prescription drugs.

- **Fighting cyber-jihad:** The alternative to infiltrating pro-jihadi websites to gather information is to set up a sting board that appears to be a forum for militant terrorism. This can be used in conjunction with infiltration to perform what has been called cyber-herding. By infiltrating known militant websites and entering the circle of trust of the terrorists, infiltrators can suggest new websites. Once the new websites are established inside the circle of trust, the original websites can be shut down and the terrorists will migrate automatically to the sting board.

- **Honeypots:** A "honeypot" is a computer that is dropped onto the internet with the sole purpose of being a "tethered goat" to attract hackers. The computer will normally have one or more known system vulnerabilities, which a hacker can exploit, once the hacker has broken into the computer everything is recorded and logged. The information gathered from a honeypot can give valuable insights into the latest attack techniques used by hackers and other cyber-criminals, including details of zero day attacks which are so new that there is no security fix. This information can be passed on to software manufacturers so that a patch for the security vulnerability can be written and distributed. Honeypots can be also be used to trap malware such as viruses and worms for later de-compilation and analysis.

  Since their inception, some time around 2002, honeypots have become very popular amongst computer security experts and companies. There is now a wide variety of software available that is relatively easy to use and virtually any moderately skilled computer user can set up a honeypot on their own computer systems. Because of the availability of honeypot software, it is impossible to tell how many honeypots are running on computers across the internet, but it is likely that there are hundreds of thousands, at least. It is impossible to tell whether a vulnerable computer is a genuine system or a honeypot – but if a vulnerable computer system seems "too good to be true", it is probably a honeypot.

  There is some debate about the ethics of using honeypots. Is it entrapment? Yet the use of entrapment techniques by law enforcement is long established – bait cars are left with the key in the ignition to trap car thieves, and police women pose as prostitutes to trap men who wish to use their services. Everybody knows that hacking a system that is not your own is illegal – just because a computer system on the internet is insecure, that does not excuse using black hat techniques to break into it. The growth of honeypots on the internet means that hackers and cyber-criminals never know if they are exploiting a real system or not, undermining their confidence and making it harder for them to remain undetected – a positive method of fighting the scourge of cybercrime.

- **Phishing Sites:** The use of phishing techniques by cyber-criminals has long been a concern for law enforcement and security experts. Phishing starts with spam – there an estimated 156 million phishing spam emails sent out across the web everyday. The spam normally contains a link to a fake website, which often appears identical to a real website. When the unsuspecting user clicks on the link to access the website, they are misdirected to the fake website. Phishing websites are normally used for two types of cyber-criminal activity. The traditional use of a phishing website is to emulate an online banking website to record the online credentials of the user. Once the cyber-criminals have the userID and login password, they can access the online banking website – and the victim's money – at any time. The other type of phishing site is used to insert malware onto the victim's computer. Normally the fake website contains a dropper which uses zero day vulnerabilities to install a banking trojan such as Zeus, (RAT) or a botnet client.

The problem with phishing websites is huge. In 2007 it was estimated that 100,000 new phishing websites are placed on the internet by cyber-criminals every week, or five million over a year[25]. To give an idea of scale of the problem, PayPal, the online payment service, is targeted by 750 new phishing sites every day, or over 270,000 per year[26]. Software add-ons for web browsers such as

25 Bogdan Popa, "100.000 New Phishing Websites Every Week", 2007, *Softpedia*
26 Eduard Kovacs, "German Email Security Provider: 750 New PayPal Phishing Sites Spotted Every Day", 2013, *Softpedia*

anti-phishing toolbars are one option, but the only real solution is user education. Only around 10 per cent of the spam sent out everyday actually gets through spam and phishing filters – and of these 16 million spam email messages around eight million emails are opened and read. Approximately 800,000 email recipients actually click on the URL embedded in the email and visit the phishing site, and of those around 80,000 users become victims of the phishing attack.

Phishing is the number one technique used by entry-level cyber-criminals. The easy availability of phishing kits make it simple for cyber-criminals to set up fake websites, even if they have little or no technical ability. Recently, to evade spam filters and anti-phishing software, cyber-criminals have started using social networking to contact their victims. As mentioned already, the Koobface gang had an estimated 20,000 fake users on Facebook allowing access to a huge number of potential victims. Users are much more likely to click on a link sent by a Facebook friend even if they have never met them. The use of high volume spam and social networks means that phishing is one of the biggest threats on the internet today and is unlikely to go away any time soon.

Conclusion

How much of a problem is the fake internet? It can be argued that the use of sock puppets, honeypots and sting boards in the fight against cybercrime and terrorism is a good thing – a low cost method of monitoring and catching criminals and terrorists. Internet users who access websites with illegal content, hackers who break into computers and terrorists sharing bomb-making manuals all know their actions are illegal. These people are *not* innocent. They have an option of not accessing the websites, but they choose to do so – and that is their downfall.

The real problem lies in the use of sock puppets for cybercrime and the vast number of phishing websites on the internet. In these cases there is no choice involved and vast amounts of innocent internet users become victims on a daily basis. When sock puppets and phishing are combined, the impact on social networking sites is huge, causing a general loss of overall confidence by the average internet user. The problem with astro turfing is also having an impact on user confidence. When messages that are pro "big oil" or pro "big pharma" get posted onto the net, nobody knows if the grassroots support is genuine or not. Undermining confidence in the internet is one of the major threats faced by the internet itself. If the general public no longer trusts the online services on the internet, what will happen to the web in the future?

16

CORPORATE MALWARE

This chapter was going to examine the growth of corporate malware, where security companies write software that in the hands of any other person would be illegal. These corporations are not writing dual use tools which can be used by security experts to make the internet safer or by criminals to commit cybercrimes. The evidence suggests that large corporations are actively involved in the development of rootkits, RATs and packages of attack tools containing multiple vulnerabilities solely designed for compromising a computer. In other words they are writing the same types of malware that cyber-criminals use on a daily basis.

But this chapter relies on a single source of information: the emails stolen from HBGary by Anonymous and published on the internet for anyone to download, replicate and use as they saw fit. The key word is stolen. This is not data supplied by an insider or whistle blower such as Bradley Manning or Edward Snowden, who copied and leaked data to Wikileaks or the media.

Anonymous used black hat hacking techniques to break into the servers of HBGary and then steal their data. How would you feel if your private emails were robbed and shared across the internet for all time? Nothing on the internet can be erased. Data can be copied and replicated forever across millions of computers. It is not like HBGary can recall a book and have all the copies pulped. Internet data is forever. When Anonymous performed the 2011 HBGary hack, they didn't just cross the line, they tried to erase it altogether. This leaves me in a dilemma. Do I write this chapter using stolen emails as my primary source? There are several reasons why I have chosen to remove this chapter and they are outlined below.

In the years between 1987 and 1995 I was heavily involved in the hacking scene. Although we were routinely entering into computers we had a hacker ethic which defined the early digital travellers: take only memories, don't damage systems or data and respect the computer and networks you were hacking on. Sometimes it was as easy as logging on with a default password. There was an old hacker joke that when you saw a computer you did not know, you should type GUEST – an abbreviation of Give Up, Stop, Exit, Terminate and type it twice to ensure you exited the computer. The problem of default passwords has not gone away, as the 2001 Gary McKinnon NASA hack proved. Wandering through those unused and quiet digital spaces in the early days of the internet was a privilege for only the few who were there at the time. Now the internet is no longer a digital village, it is a sprawling metropolis.

> **The HBGary emails are tainted data and although anybody can download them from the internet it doesn't change the fact that they were stolen.**

What I never did was use social engineering attacks that manipulated people into telling me passwords. Most hackers who use social engineering will read the email on the system, either looking for passwords or the identity of somebody who they can impersonate. I never read anyone's email because it seemed like a betrayal of privacy – not unlike opening somebody's mail without permission, or reading a secret diary. I enjoyed the technical challenges in hacking, the freedom of roaming the early internet and being a part of the underground hacking community. I also never stole personal data, although I confess that the publically available UNIX password file would sometimes get copied for the express purpose of cracking the passwords, but this was readable by everyone on the computer and was not private data. The theft and publication of the HBGary emails is thus against my personal hacker code.

Secondly, when I write a book I like to use open source information which is freely available to anyone who chooses to check my research. I use books and newspapers, but most of all I use the internet, which means that the majority of information that has been used is available to anybody who searched the internet. What I never use is insider information, informants, stolen documents, hacking techniques or phone hacking. The HBGary emails are tainted data, and although anybody can download them from the internet it doesn't change the fact that they were stolen.

Thirdly, I have doubts about the legality of writing a chapter based entirely on stolen data. The possession of the data could be interpreted as a crime. It could leave both myself and the publisher open to charges that we were co-conspirators with Anonymous by using and distributing a chapter based on the HBGary emails. We don't even know if the contents of the HBGary emails are real. Digital information is changeable and replicable, and the exfiltration of the emails of a high-level security company allow for digital *maskirovka* at the highest level. At any point somebody could have changed the stolen emails and released them on the internet with the express purpose of causing as much embarrassment to HBGary as possible. If the data were later found to be false, then myself and the publisher could be accused of being dupes or useful idiots by taking the HBGary emails at face value and relying on them as a primary source. The possible repercussions of publishing the data outweigh the importance of this information.

So even if the stolen HBGary emails provide a unique insight into the development of corporate malware, the nature of the data and the way it was obtained prevents it from being used. Of course, any reader can use Google to research the matter for themselves and draw their own conclusions.

It is important to note that there is a difference between whistleblowers who uncover government or corporate malfeasance by leaking documents in their possession and the digital theft and mass distribution of documents from a third party.

17

PERPETUAL SURVEILLANCE SOCIETY

During the Cold War the differences between the competing global powers blocs were easily defined. The enemy was perceived to be communists, in particular the USSR and China, but also proxy states such as Cuba or North Korea, which fell under the communist sphere of influence. Back at the height of the Cold War (1953–1962), the USA wanted to intercept the communications of their enemies, decrypt their codes and inject false information into the system. In some ways, nothing has changed, the struggle continues between the power blocs, as we have seen already, but some of the names have been changed. With the collapse of communism in 1989 and the economic liberation of China, the world should be entering a new era of peace, but the events of September 11, 2001 shattered any post-Cold War optimism.

To understand the growth of the modern perpetual surveillance society, we need to remember that the idea of surveillance is not new. In the twentieth-century the Gestapo (across Nazi-occupied Europe), the KGB (across the Soviet Union), and the Stasi (across East Germany) struck fear into peoples hearts and were all tools of oppression that used surveillance techniques to facilitate state control. This is the hunt for the enemy within, for moles, spies, terrorists, and dissidents who threaten the apparatus of state control.

But 9/11 changed all that. It redefined the enemy within to the point that innocent people are now considered suspects. This goes beyond the data-mining efforts of the DEA and FBI to catch drug traffickers, money-launderers and RICO-based conspirators. This targets ordinary people. Anybody could end up on a secret government blacklist and become a perpetual suspect who warrants continual surveillance forever.

Is the new model of perpetual surveillance just something that has grown out of the post 9/11 paranoia and the US' "War on Terror"? The answer is no. The USA have always engaged the possibility of the "enemy within" and waged a constant war against them. In 1908, the US government formed the "Bureau of Investigation" (BOI) to investigate anarchist activities on US soil. Later, the BOI investigated German agents who were working for the Kaiser before and during World War I. In 1935, the BOI was renamed as the Federal Bureau of Investigation and the FBI, as we know it today, was born.

Although famous for the crime-busting tactics that targeted organized crime, from its very inception the FBI had another purpose, to hunt for the "enemy within". In 1935 the threat was from spies and agents of Nazi Germany who were operating with impunity in the USA. By the end of the World War II, the focus had

Anybody could end up on a secret government blacklist and become a perpetual suspect who warrants continual surveillance forever.

changed. With the onset of the Cold War the "enemy within" was redefined as communist agents who were suspected to be in the pay of Moscow and Peking. As the Cold War progressed, the FBI added new targets to their list of suspects: groups such as the civil rights movement, protesters against the Vietnam War, and "new left" groups such as "Students for a Democratic Society" (SDS) were all targeted for surveillance. It is therefore known that the techniques of surveillance used against the "enemy within" have been part of American society for over a century. What has changed are two things: 1) the redefinition of the "enemy within" as "radical Islam" and its fellow travellers and, 2) the rapid growth of a technology that can be harnessed for modern perpetual surveillance, also known as the "internet".

The NSA, formed in 1952, was once so secret that insiders joked that NSA stood for "No Such Agency". The role of the NSA is the monitoring, decoding and analysis of electronic information from a variety of satellites, undersea cables and the internet to support US intelligence operations. This form of intelligence is called signals intelligence (SIGINT) and can be contrasted with the human intelligence (HUMINT) gathered by the CIA. The NSA is the primary source for all signals intelligence in the USA. Staff numbers are classified but have been estimated to be around 40,000, and with a budget of over $10 billion (£6.2 billion), it is one of the largest intelligence agencies in the world.

The equivalent organization in the UK is the Government Communications Headquarters (GCHQ). Founded in 1919, and called the Government Code and Cypher School, this signals intelligence unit was responsible for breaking the Nazi Enigma code during World War II. After the end of the second World War it was renamed as GCHQ. It works closely with the NSA, and it seems likely that both organizations share their data. This has the benefit of allowing the NSA access to data collected by the UK on US nationals without any possibility of legal oversight. Both the NSA and CIA are legally not allowed to spy on US citizens without a warrant, so the use of outsourcing allows plausible deniability, while still allowing US agencies access to data on US citizens.

There is a growing trend towards the semi-privatization of intelligence gathering across the planet. This is the "outsourcing" of digital intelligence, where proxy actors (such as the UK) can collect huge amount of meta-data on the behavior of another country's citizens. In 2013, it was reported that the NSA paid GCHQ somewhere in the region of $100 million (£62 million) for access to this data over the last three years. According to the NSA whistle blower Edward Snowden, the NSA paid GCHQ £22.9 million in 2009, £39.9 million in 2010 and £34.7 million in 2011/12.

It has long been known that Australia, Canada, New Zealand, the United Kingdom, and the United States have been using a signals collection and analysis network to intercept commercial satellite communications. The **ECHELON** program, started in the early 1960s at the height of the Cold War, was built to enable the easy monitoring of military and diplomatic traffic emanating from the Eastern Bloc. It has been alleged that Echelon was capable of sifting through and inspecting the content of everything passed across the satellite links, including telephone calls, fax, email and other traffic across the telephone networks.

In the modern world, fiber-optical cables have replaced many satellite links that should make communications more secure. However, it has been alleged that both the USA and the UK have placed interception "taps" on undersea fiber optic cables. Whether this is true or not remains to be seen. It is much easier to place a tap on the landward side of the cable, enabling access to all the information flowing through the "fat pipe" linking the US and UK networks together. We do know that one of the leaked PRISM slides refers to the upstream collection of communications on fiber cables and infrastructure as data flows past, via several processes with the code names Fairview, Stormbrew, Blarney and Oakstar. These are likely to be the names of major collection points that tap into the data pipes. A recent report suggests that GCHQ have tapped over 200 fiber optic cables in an operation codenamed **Tempora**. The website of the German paper *Süddeutsche Zeitung* has published the names of several of the fiber optic cables tapped by GCHQ:

- TAT–14, connecting the United States with the UK, France, the Netherlands, Germany, and Denmark
- Atlantic Crossing 1 (AC–1), linking the USA and the UK, the Netherlands and Germany
- Sea–Me–We 3, which connects Europe, Asia and the Middle East
- Sea–Me–We 4, linking Europe, North Africa and Asia
- FLAG Europe Asia (FEA), linking Europe to Japan through the Middle East and India
- FLAG Atlantic-1, linking New York with France and England
- Circe North, connecting the UK with Belgium, France, Germany and the Netherlands
- Circe South, connecting the UK with Belgium, France, Germany and the Netherlands
- Solas, between the UK and Ireland across the Irish Sea
- UK–France 3
- UK–Netherlands 14
- Ulysses 1 and 2, running between Dover to Ijmuiden, Netherlands, and Calais to Lowestoft
- Yellow/AC–2, connecting New York with Bude, UK
- Pan European Crossing (PEC), linking the UK, Belgium, and France

As can be seen from the leaked PRISM diagram, much of the world's communications flow through the USA. Total available global bandwidth is 12,383 gigabits per second(Gbps) and the bandwidth of the USA is 10,650 Gbps. From that we can see that the US accounts for 86 per cent of the total available global bandwidth. Because of the way the global network functions, an email, phone call or chat will always take the cheapest path and not the most direct path. This means that there is a very good chance that the target's communications could be flowing into and through the USA.

In the post-9/11 period, the NSA began a program of electronic surveillance called the Terrorist Surveillance Program. By 2005, it had become apparent that the techniques used by the NSA could, and often did, infringe on the rights of US citizens by collecting their phone data. George W. Bush also approved a new intelligence gathering effort called the President's Surveillance Program (PSP). The code name for this was Stellar Wind and consisted of four different surveillance programs that targeted non-US nationals. Although it was alleged to have finished in 2004, the four programs eventually resurfaced during the PRISM revelations in 2013. The four programs are:

MAINWAY

By 2011 it was alleged that the NSA had begun storing all phone billing records for everyone in the country. MAINWAY is a massive database containing detailed telephone call data – e.g. caller, receiver, timing details etc. It is believed that the MAINWAY database contains over 1.9 trillion call records, made through the largest phone companies in the USA. These records are kept for up to five years. It is estimated that the MAINWAY system stores around 1.8 billion phone call records, made every day.

MARINA

MARINA is the main database for storing internet meta-data. It provides a record of almost everything an internet user does online; including browsing history, account details, email activity, and even some account passwords. This data is stored for a year, allowing intelligence analysts to look back in time when somebody is a suspect, but it also stores the data from vast numbers of innocent people.

NUCLEON

The NUCLEON program intercepts telephone calls and then strips out the content, which is sent to a database for later inspection or data mining.

PRISM

In the summer of 2013 the newspapers the *Washington Post* and *Guardian* began to publish a series of articles based on leaked documentation about the true scope of NSA data-mining projects. The 41 leaked slides were intended for senior analysts in the NSA's Signals Intelligence Directorate.

It later transpired that the whistle blower who gave the slides to the media was Edward Snowden, a former employee of the CIA and NSA, who decided to release the details of the NSA surveillance programs to the public because he was "disillusioned about the amount of information the US was able to collect from emails, phone records and credit cards and saw it as an infringement of people's civil liberties." Snowdon has said: "I do not want to live in a world where everything I do and say is recorded." After revealing his identity, Edward Snowden left the USA and is currently in Russia, having been granted political asylum. The US government, needless to say, are not happy about his role in the PRISM revelations, and he is currently charged with theft of government property, unauthorized communication of national defence information, and willful communication of classified intelligence to an unauthorized person. The fact that Edward Snowden appears to have defected to Russia does nothing to allay the suspicions of agencies that remember the Cold War. We have not seen such a high-profile defection since the end of the Cold War, and it seems unlikely that Edward Snowden will ever set foot in the USA ever again.

The PRISM system, opposite, seems complicated at first glance, but it is actually quite simple. The module PRINTAURA automates traffic flow and requests for data. The SCISSORS and PROTOCOL EXPLOITATION modules organize the incoming data types for analysis and passes the data to the correct module: NUCLEON for voice, PINWALE for video, MAINWAY for phone records and MARINA for internet **metadata**. It has been speculated that the modules called FALLOUT and CONVEYANCE are filtering modules designed to cut down on the information gathered on US citizens. It has also been speculated that TRAFFICTHIEF is a sub-module that deals with known persons of interest by diverting the data collected on known suspects to a different database. The PRISM program allows for high-level access to both live online communications and information stored in various databases. According to the slides leaked by Edward Snowden, many of the largest internet companies are allowing the NSA direct access to their servers for purposes of data-mining, and have done so for many years.

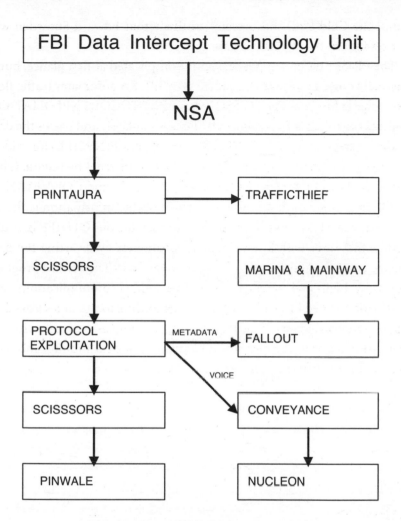

The data flow of the PRISM programming
Source: Snowden Leaks (2013)

Here is a list of the internet companies alleged to have participated in PRISM and the dates they joined the program.

- 2007   Microsoft
- 2008   Yahoo
- 2009   Google, Facebook, PalTalk
- 2010   YouTube
- 2011   Skype, AOL
- 2012   Apple

What kind of data does PRISM collect? Just about everything:

- Email
- Chat (video, text, voice)
- Videos
- Photos
- Stored data
- VoIP data (e.g. Skype)
- File transfers
- Video conferencing
- Activities (e.g. logging in or logging out)
- Social networking details (e.g. Facebook, LinkdIn, MySpace etc)
- Special Requests (e.g. covert digital warfare or cyberwar)

PRISM goes beyond the collection of meta-data. It allows the collection of the actual content of *everything that happens* on the internet. There is one curious addition to this list, Special Requests. One wonders what this could mean. Does it mean "digital black bag jobs" that install government approved malware such as a RATs. With the current growth in the technology of cyber weaponry, it can be speculated that Special Requests means digital special operations – i.e. covert digital warfare or cyberwar, but the true nature of Special Requests is unknown at this time.

Although internet companies are required to give up data to law enforcement officials when they issue a warrant or subpoena, the claims about PRISM go far beyond the types of activities that require normal legal oversight. They claim that the NSA has direct access to the servers that provide vast portions of the web with useful services. When the *Guardian* newspaper contacted the companies concerned, they responded with these denials:

Apple: "We have never heard of PRISM. We do not provide any government agency with direct access to our servers and any agency requesting customer data must get a court order."

Facebook: "When Facebook is asked for data or information about specific individuals, we carefully scrutinize any such request for compliance with all applicable laws, and provide information only to the extent required by law."

Google: "Google cares deeply about the security of our users' data. We disclose user data to government in accordance with the law, and we review all such requests carefully. From time to time, people allege that we have created a government 'backdoor' into our systems, but Google does not have a 'back door' for the government to access private user data."

Microsoft: "We provide customer data only when we receive a legally binding order or subpoena to do so, and never on a voluntary basis. In addition we only ever comply with orders for requests about specific accounts or identifiers. If the government has a broader voluntary national security program to gather customer data we don't participate in it."

Yahoo!: "Yahoo! takes users' privacy very seriously. We do not provide the government with direct access to our servers, systems, or network."

In fact nobody admitted knowing anything about the PRISM program. Every company on the list claimed that there was no NSA direct access to their servers, and that they provided data only when presented with a court order or subpoena. How then is this possible? The companies deny allowing the NSA access to their servers, but at the same time the slides from the NSA clearly show that these companies are co-operating with the NSA in the data collection process. Here are some possibilities of why these companies have taken the stance they have towards PRISM:

Possibility One

The companies are co-operating with the NSA but are denying all knowledge of the PRISM program due to national security concerns.

Possibility Two

The NSA are tapping into ISPs with black boxes that filter all data coming from and going to the websites run by these internet giants. ISPs are likely to comply with government requests for locally based internet meta-data, and maybe even content data when issued with a warrant. Collecting this data and placing it into a huge database and data-mining for connections would produce the type of data that PRISM allegedly contains.

Possibility Three

The NSA are using upstream analysis by exploiting internet choke points through which large amounts of internet traffic flows. Then the NSA can tap into a wealth of data, which it can include in their databases. The problem with this is that one of the leaked slides clearly recommends using both upstream analysis and PRISM, so we can conclude that both types of data gathering operations exist.

There is another possibility. It is known that the NSA receive access to zero day vulnerabilities by Microsoft even before a security patch has been written. It is also known that the NSA purchase zero day vulnerabilities on the open market. The only purpose of zero day vulnerabilities is to exploit computer system vulnerabilities and obtain illicit access. Are the NSA hacking into the servers of these internet companies in order to gain access?

If this sounds far-fetched, then consider the recent proposals that the NSA should be should be allowed to make computer assurance security checks on software to ensure that it is secure. There are, of course, several problems with this course of action. Would you trust the NSA to make these checks? Would you trust the NSA to secure your data? These are some of the possible reasons why the NSA should not be trusted to perform quality control checks on software.

- Would the NSA publish their findings so that independent security researchers could verify the NSA testing results?
- Can the NSA guarantee that all the bugs they find will be fixed – or will they keep them secret so that they can gain access to any computer running that OS and software combination?

- Can the NSA guarantee not to insert backdoors in the form of vulnerabilities into the program they are analyzing?

It sounds like paranoia, but we know that the NSA are researching computer insecurity techniques to facilitate their intelligence programs. There is already a school of thought that alleges the NSA are working actively with major software providers to program backdoors into commonly used software and operating systems. Given the state of the art in software design, these backdoors are likely to take the form of vulnerabilities that can only be exploited by state of the art buffer overflow attacks. The major problems with backdoors is that any skilled hacker or cyber-criminal can also find these vulnerabilities. Allowing backdoors into any computer system makes it more insecure, and if many computers have backdoors, then the security of the entire internet is under threat.

Boundless Informant

According to revelations made by Edward Snowdon in 2013, Boundless Informant is an NSA data-mining tool that maps (by country) the meta-data that the NSA collects. The focus of Boundless Informant is on countries and the categorization of communications, rather than the actual content of email, Skype, VoIP or telephone calls. This is pure Signals Intelligence (SIGINT) using **traffic analysis**. By ignoring the content of the information, and concentrating on the origins and destinations of the traffic, the NSA is able to use Social Networking Analysis (SNA) to build models that show the flow of communications between individuals. The documents leaked by Snowden suggest that over three billion pieces of information were collected from US computer networks over a mere 30 days in 2013. Worldwide, the same 30-day period saw around 97 billion pieces of information collected by the NSA.

The countries targeted should be no surprise. The Boundless Informan program scooped up billions of pieces data from the following countries: Iran, 14 billion; Pakistan, 13.5 billion; Jordan,12.7 billion; Egypt, 7.6 billion; and India, 6.3 billion. The data collected includes IP meta-data, which could indicate country, state, city and possible location of internet users. Without inspecting the content, emails can be examined for the sender and recipient. The phone data includes time, duration, caller and number-dialled. Of, course, data from cellular phones can also include meta-data designed to be used internally by the phone company, i.e. the current cell tower being used, allowing movement tracking even when GPS is disabled. It appears that Boundless Informant is a powerful tool for recording and analyzing meta-data of all kinds, and that the NSA call record database is possibly the largest database in the world.

Phone Tapping

While Boundless Informant is mostly aimed at foreign nationals, it is now known that the NSA collects millions of US customer records such as location data, call duration, the time of calls, and unique identifiers used by the telephone company for routing information. As the American Civil Liberties Union (ACLU) points out, "it allows the government to build a profile which can reveal political and religious associations, medical conditions, infidelities and more". Meta-data can be as sensitive as content – who you are talking to, for how long, who calls you and maybe even the location you are calling from.

But this is not new. According to a recent article in *The New York Times* law enforcement officials who are fighting the War on Drugs have had access to a huge database of call records dating back to 1987 from the telephone company AT&T. These records include every call that passes through the AT&T phone network, and not just those of their customers. It is alleged that the database has four billion new records added every day. The data is used to trace patterns in the use of prepaid burner phones used by drug dealers, but the meta-data can reveal patterns of call behavior that is useful in building evidence against criminals. A drug dealer that changes phones but remains in the same location and makes a continual pattern of calls to the same number can be watched and evidence can be obtained. Unlike the NSA, this data is actually owned by AT&T. Access to the data base is only given to law enforcement officials with a subpoena, and even then there are AT&T officials who assist agents in sifting through the vast amount of data.

XKeyscore

Xkeyscore (XKS) is an NSA program designed to exploit the massive databases at their disposal, and it is claimed that the program covers "nearly everything a user does on the internet".[1] It is claimed that the program can intercept and monitor a target's internet activity in real time, generating intelligence from network activity. This "Digital Network Intelligence" program allows analysts to read the content of Facebook chats and private messages, and also determine the IP address of any visitor to a targeted website. The amount of data stored is huge. In 2012, it was estimated that XKeyscore collected 41 billion records in a 30-day period.

The NSA insists that by 2008, 300 terrorists had been captured using intelligence gathered from XKeyscore.[27]

This suggests that NSA data-capturing and data-mining efforts make us safer. However, the noted security expert Bruce Schneier has investigated this issue and has arrived at some startling conclusions. Schneier points out that data-mining works best when agents search for something matching a particular profile – for example, credit card fraud where purchases and spending patterns could indicate a stolen credit card. He then goes on to argue that terrorist plots, which have no well-defined profiles, are different and that until data-mining techniques are highly accurate, they are doomed to failure. As Schneier observes in his article "Why Data Mining Won't Stop Terror", *Wired* magazine, 2006:

> All data-mining systems fail in two different ways: false positives and false negatives. A false positive is when the system identifies a terrorist plot that really isn't one. A false negative is when the system misses an actual terrorist plot. Depending on how you "tune" your detection algorithms, you can err on one side or the other: you can increase the number of false positives to ensure you are less likely to miss an actual terrorist plot, or you can reduce the number of false positives at the expense of missing terrorist plots.

27 Glenn Greenwald, "XKeyscore: NSA tool collects 'nearly everything a user does on the internet'", 2013, *The Guardian*

Schneier then goes on to look at some numbers and makes a startling discovery:

> We'll be optimistic – we'll assume the system has a one in 100 false-positive rate (99 per cent accurate), and a one in 1,000 false-negative rate (99.9 per cent accurate). Assume one trillion possible indicators to sift through: that's about 10 events – e-mails, phone calls, purchases, web destinations, whatever – per person in the United States per day. Also assume that 10 of them are actually terrorists plotting.
>
> This unrealistically accurate system will generate one billion false alarms for every real terrorist plot it uncovers. Every day of every year, the police will have to investigate 27 million potential plots in order to find the one real terrorist plot per month. Raise that false-positive accuracy to an absurd 99.9999 per cent and you're still chasing 2,750 false alarms per day – but that will inevitably raise your false negatives, and you're going to miss some of those 10 real plots.[28]

Schneier concludes that the government would be "better off putting people in charge of investigating potential plots and letting them direct the computers instead of putting the computers in charge and letting them decide who should be investigated."

This is the problem with data-mining in a nutshell. Looking for terrorist plots is like looking for a needle in a haystack and the haystack just keeps getting bigger and bigger. The use of artificial intelligence and data-mining techniques on huge databases, which contain billions and billions of records of innocent people, inevitably leads to people being wrongfully watched or even arrested.

28 Bruce Schneier, "Why Data Mining Won't Stop Terror", *Wired* magazine, 2006

Conclusion

The future looks bleak, but it could soon get bleaker. There are rumors of a new NSA initiative called Project Avatar. Project Avatar seeks to create a profile for every man, woman and child on the planet. Once established, data flowing from a number of sources will be added to the files. Everything from credit records, purchases, phone usage, internet usage and more will be added to the unique profile of every individual. When the database is complete it will be possible to choose any individual and learn everything about them a matter of minutes. The databases used in the PRISM program outlined above will be an important part of Project Avatar, but other databases can be purchased on the open market. Once a profile is established and a person becomes a terrorist suspect, their profile can be matched against other profiles in an attempt to locate other possible terrorist suspects. As discussed, this type of profiling will inevitably target innocent people.

The growth of the automated perpetual surveillance society is one of the largest modern threats that our democratic civilization faces today. Are we exchanging our expectation of privacy to an expectation of perpetual surveillance? The use of automated AI programs to determine potential suspects is a modern day version of Franz Kafka's *The Trial* (1925), where anyone could be accused of anything and not even know that they have been accused. The digital panopticon has arrived, and we are all "volunteering" to be watched. What can we do to prevent ourselves from being watched? As we shall see in the next chapter, going "off the grid" is not an option, as the very act of going "off the grid" is suspicious.

18

DIGITAL PARANOIA

Over the last 20 years there has been an increasing awareness of cyber threat. Fifteen years ago when I wrote the first edition of *Hackers' Handbook*, the threat landscape was different. The major threat was hobbyist hackers – computer geeks who colonized cyberspace and made it their own. It was relatively easy to secure your computer because the threat level was so much lower.

But hacking is no fun anymore. Not only because the chances of getting caught are much higher, but because cyberspace itself has been re-colonized by a different breed of hacker. Nowadays, cybercrime is the number one preoccupation for all hackers, followed by the threat of cyber-hacktivists and cyber-terrorists. Meanwhile, nation state actors are gearing up for cyberwar and developing the tools and weapons that will impact all of our lives if cyberwar breaks out.

The emerging new levels of threat are one of the reasons why I attempted to go "off the grid". I figured that not having an internet connection, a smartphone, or a credit card would protect me against the major internet threats of the modern age. Going off the grid seemed like a smart move.

As it turned out, I was wrong. Just because I am paranoid it does not mean they aren't out to get me. The growth in modern data-mining and automated surveillance techniques actually make it more likely that I will be profiled as a suspect. In this chapter I will turn the spotlight on myself and come to a startling conclusion. My behavior makes me a potential terrorist suspect. The result being that I could become a person of interest. Everything I do online will be watched. The consequences would be horrific – it would destroy my life as well as impact the lives of my family and friends.

What are the Potential Indicators of Terrorist Activities? According to the DHS and FBI there are many. Luckily I don't have missing fingers, chemical-stained hands or buy suspicious chemicals in bulk. I don't hang-out photographing potential attack sites nor do I make violent anti-American statements. But what is left is more than enough to build my personal terrorist profile.

Financial Data-Mining

It is well known that the USA has been data-mining and recording financial transactions via the Society for Worldwide Interbank Financial Telecommunications (SWIFT) who also monitor credit card transactions and bank accounts. Just paying off your credit card bill in a single swoop can bring you a visit from Homeland Security – as the innocent Walter Soehnge found to his cost in 2006, and mentioned earlier in the book. Being "off the grid" means that I have no transactions – an act which is suspicious in itself. There is no record of a mortgage in my name, nor a rental agreement, because I own the house I live in. There is no record of any credit card payments in my name because I do not own a credit card or even a debit card. Yet using cash for commercial transactions without a credit card is a suspicious activity in itself. These days living within your means and insisting on paying with cash is an indicator of a possible crime.

Driving Licence

Everybody needs a valid ID for many routine transactions and the de-facto form of ID is the driving license. It so happens that I do not have a driving license. Not because of illness or an driving offence, but because when I was growing up I was too much of a tech-geek to bother. While my peers were learning to drive I spent all my time reading science fiction and learning how to program. As I grew older, raising a family and a busy academic career took precedence and in London the public transport is better than car ownership anyway. But to an outside observer this is all very strange behavior. For the automated systems that monitor our lives not having a driving license means that I am either (a) not who I say I am or (b) an eco-freak who hates cars. Not having a driving license is a potential indicator of terrorist activity, once again making me a possible "person of interest".

Facebook Contacts

Since the PRISM revelations of 2013 we know that the NSA monitor social networking sites such as Facebook, but what do they look for?

By using Social Network Analysis (SNA) the NSA can figure out every users friendship networks. If you get connected to the wrong person then you can be profiled as a person of interest. But how hard is it to be incorrectly profiled? It has been theorized that anyone in the world can be connected to anyone else in the world by just "six degrees of separation" –the idea that chains of friends of friends can be used to connect anyone in the world.

But we know that the NSA are routinely monitoring social networks such as Facebook and that they allegedly explore up to three degrees of separation when investigating social networks. Do they dig deeper? We don't know. What is known is that the average link between any two randomly chosen people on Facebook – a highly dense social networking site with 99.91 per cent of interconnection – has increased the likelihood of connection between those two randomly chosen people to 4.74 degrees of separation.[29]

My contacts on Facebook are a mixed bunch and they include people from various backgrounds that could suggest terrorist links. Just because someone was born in a country alleged to form part of the "axis of evil" does not make them a terrorist. However if their name is similar to somebody that is already a person of interest then they could be investigated. Worse still, the degrees of separation theory almost certainly guarantees that somebody I know knows somebody who knows somebody

29 Barnett, Emma (22 November 2011). "Facebook Cuts Six Degrees of Separation to Four". *Telegraph*. Retrieved 7 May 2012.

who could already be profiled as a terrorist. Dig deeper and you find the link between many of my friends is simple – we went to the same university – which had a reputation as a hotbed of left-wing agitation and possible links with the left wing terrorist "Angry Brigade" group in the UK. Do I look suspicious yet?

Google Searches

What do my Google searches reveal about me? These days my Google searches are highly refined, highly specialized and tightly focused on digital warfare, counter terrorism and future technological warfare such as EMP weapons and SCADA attacks. In fact the searches made through Google are so specific that they are made either by a terrorist or an independent researcher writing about terrorism. The automated AI based data-mining engines of the NSA do not know the difference. All these systems know is that my pattern of searches matches the profile of a typical terrorist. Once again, although I have nothing to hide I have everything to fear, the very act of researching this book has possibly brought me to the attention of the perpetual surveillance society and made me a potential suspect. The heightened level of digital paranoia was in the news recently when a young couple in the USA were visited by a law enforcement agency with the joint terrorism task force after Googling for the words "pressure cooker" and "backpacks". Many security experts speculated that the Google searches were picked up by the NSA PRISM program that routinely monitors all internet traffic but the truth was more mundane. A company had discovered evidence of the searches on a work computer and then called the police, who acting on the tip off, investigated the couple and found nothing untoward. This is the virtual fear of the modern world – who has access to the data that could be misinterpreted by modern automated surveillance systems? We don't know. But we do know we are perpetually watched by machines that – as we all know – can be wrong from time to time.

Shared Links

So what happens if I use a social networking site for link sharing and post links about cyber-terrorism and counter-intelligence for others to see? Under UK law it is illegal to post material that promotes terrorism. But this is the raw material most useful for any researcher interested in the field. Crawling the links provided on this type of website is easy and anyone can do it. When this information is added to the mass of information already available from Google and Facebook once again it fits the profile of a terrorist. If the links posted on a social networking site are deemed to be promoting terrorism the government can ask the service provider to remove the offending page. In a single stroke my account could be withdrawn and my entire online life, my contacts with friends and family could be taken away from me.

Cell phone surveillance

Being "off the grid" means I have no phone line – but I do have a cell phone. Cell phones are the ultimate location tracking devices in the world. Even if you disable GPS, the very fact that cell phones handover from one cell tower to another as you move means that location tracking is easy. Calls are monitored and saved, voicemail exists on a server somewhere and even if you delete all of your texts and saved details specialist software can recover the data from your SIM.

But suppose you never carry your phone? My phone sits on the shelf, it is hardly ever used and is rarely remembered when I leave the house. Last time I looked it was covered in dust. What would the automated surveillance systems conclude about such behavior? It is likely that the low level of incoming and outgoing calls and the lack of movement would lead such systems to conclude that I was using an untraceable "burner phone" rather than the one registered in my name. There is a pattern of usage that normal users display when using a cell phone – and I do not fit that pattern. In fact I can't remember when I last used it. This is yet another reason for my profile to be flagged as abnormal – warranting special attention as a person of interest.

Overseas Travel

Does my history of foreign travel raise any red flags? The fact that I have travelled to the Indian sub-continent not just once but five times in the last 15 years is an indicator of suspicion. Why would anyone travel to India five times if not for some purpose? Further digging will reveal that I have also been to a country that is known as a hotbed of Islamic fundamentalism – Egypt.

Suspicious counter-terrorist experts would naturally wonder who I met and for what reason I went. Of course, further digging would reveal everything – the trains I booked, the money I changed and even the hotels I stayed in. In India, as with many countries in Europe too, registration with a passport is a requirement in the majority of hotels and is routinely enforced by the police who check the hotel register for unregistered guests. In some towns a traveller is also required to register at the local police station. In Egypt the hotel actually took my passport and locked it in the hotel safe until it was time for me to leave. In the modern world some, or maybe even all, of this information is going to end up being encoded in a computer database somewhere in cyberspace.

Strange Patterns of Internet Usage

No internet at home? That looks suspicious, maybe. Home internet is a risk. Home internet is a permanent threat. So I use the internet for less than 30 minutes a day and that is enough. I use the internet in various locations. It takes less than 15 minutes to connect to my friends and family on a daily basis. Using different cyber café internet connections is a suspicious activity. Why not use the same one every day? Do I have something to hide?

No Fly list

Can I fly to the USA? I have no idea – the only way to find out is to try. Problems with the US "No Fly" lists, as indeed with other nations, have been known for years. It has been alleged that the secret blacklists used to prevent terrorists flying in the USA have been manipulated for political purposes to make life difficult for political opponents. If your name is similar or identical to a name on the "No Fly" list then travel becomes a hellish nightmare especially if you are only two years old. Nobody knows exactly how many names are on the "No Fly" list – somewhere between 20,000 and 100,000 – but the lists are secret and almost impossible to remove your name from. Consider this: my name is not very common but there are over 400 people with that name on Facebook last time I checked.

Computer Files

So if I become a person of interest – and my computer was hacked or searched – what would law enforcement find? A huge number of files that would be flagged as suspicious. Material with a content of a radical nature, documents about military counter-insurgency, terrorist tactics, revolutionary politics and radical literature about COINTELPRO operations, press coverage of terrorism, hacktivism and cybercrime and a whole slew of government documents. The fact that everything on my hard drive is open source material from the web is irrelevant – the sum of all the documents matches the profile of a terrorist. Worse yet, there is no pornography on my hard drive. When the police busted "Irhabi007" one of the first things that made them suspicious is that there was no pornography on his hard drive.

Conclusion

The conclusion from all this is simple. If I want to avoid suspicion, I can't be off the grid. I need to get a mortgage, a credit card, a driving license and stop paying cash for everything. I should holiday in Spain instead of India or Egypt. I should carry my cell phone with the GPS enabled at all times so that I can be tracked with ease. I shouldn't stay in touch with my friends on Facebook. I should give up writing about perpetual surveillance society because using Google and downloading certain documents make it more likely that I will be profiled as a "person of interest".

SECTION 4

CYBER-PROTECTION

"As the world is increasingly interconnected, everyone shares the responsibility of securing cyberspace."

Newton Lee, leading computer scientist

As we become evermore reliant on the exchange of electronic information, the risk of cyber attack will only ever increase. Faced with this terrifying prospect, this next section asks what can we do to protect ourselves and what does the future hold for the internet? Although cyberspace will never be totally secure, certain measures can be taken to reduce our exposure to potential danger.

19

MINIMIZING CYBER THREAT

This should be the chapter of the book where the reader learns about how to defeat cyber threats – but it's not. Cyber threat cannot be ignored, but it cannot be beaten either. We live in an age of cyber-threat but we must learn to live with it or go offline and live in a cave.

There is a problem with current models of cyber-security – and we ignore them at our peril. The sad reality is that the average zero day threat goes undetected for almost a year. Only once captured by anti-malware researchers and decompiled can this new vector of cyber attack be examined and the true nature of the cyber threat analyzed and evaluated. Then the company needs to write a fix or a "patch" for the security vulnerability, issue it or distribute updated software. This could take weeks, or even months, just to issue the software upgrade.

Then there is the patch problem. It takes around 21 days to upgrade and patch 50 per cent of corporate *servers* but it takes 62 days to patch 50 per cent of corporate desktop *computers*. Of course, some are never patched at all. Home computer users are even worse: it is estimated that over 40 per cent of the current computers attached to the internet are at risk – simply because users never download and install current computer upgrades.

What is important for internet computer security is for ordinary computer users to recognize that it is their responsibility to make their computer safer. Local computer security equates to global computer security. Securing your computer makes your network neighborhood safer. Be a good neighbor and scan your computer for malware today.

Unsecured computers represent low-hanging fruit to evil internet users – of whatever type. By securing your own computer, you can become part of the solution and not part of the problem. If you allow your computer to be infected with malware, it could become part of a botnet and then spread malware to everyone who connects to you – with horrible consequences. For this reason, every "ordinary" internet user has a responsibility to ensure that their computer is secure as possible. Here's how:

Update Your Operating System

It is a sad fact of life that 33 per cent of all the computers attached to the net are using Windows XP – but by April 2014 XP they will not supported by Microsoft and there will no longer be any upgrades or patches. If cyber-criminals find new vulnerabilities in Windows XP, they will be there forever and your computer will always be at risk. Upgrade to a modern operating system and you will receive upgrades and security patches – for a few years at least – until your new shiny modern operating system becomes obsolete also.

Use A Different Operating System

Because Microsoft possess a huge market share, the majority of malware is written for those operating systems. Using OS/X or Linux will reduce the possibilities of malware infection considerably. Due to the popularity of Microsoft Windows, the majority of malware is written for that operating system, but in the last few years banking trojans and worms have appeared for both the Linux and Macintosh platforms. Using a Z80 CP/M operating system reduces your chance of infection to near-zero. If there is a trade-off to be made, between security and convenience, always choose security. Modern technology comes at a price and that price is the responsibility of securing your own system.

Update Frequently

The first rule of computer security states that every piece of software can be exploited by a well-crafted cyber attack. The software on your computer can be used to subvert your computer itself, which is then converted into a dangerous zombie that threatens everybody on the internet. Software companies sometimes issue new versions of their software when they become aware of computer vulnerabilities. Larger corporations and organizations, which make and distribute the software we use on a daily basis, issue upgrades and patches for operating systems and software. Use the update option built into your operating system and software. Updated software should be safer and more secure than older software. Ensure you update your browser (Firefox, Chrome, Internet Explorer, etc.), and plugins (Flash, Java, QuickTime, etc.) whenever a new update is available.

Use Anti-malware Software

Whatever operating systems you choose, you need anti-virus, anti-spyware and anti-botnet software. How much you spend depends on how much you value your computer security and data, but it should be noted that there is a huge amount of free and trial anti-malware programs that are excellent. Microsoft users also have free access to state-of-the-art anti-malware programs if they are properly registered and have a supported operating system.

Use A Firewall

Firewalls block forbidden communications between your computer and the outside world – minimizing the risk that malware can communicate with the internet. Firewalls will not stop all cyber threats because they can still allow malware to infect your computer through an open HTTP connection by using zero day exploits, malware PDF files and other vectors of attack via client-side vulnerabilities. But at least cyber scum will not be able to discover so much information about your computer. Anything inside your browser could be a threat – despite using a firewall – because you have permitted the connection. Web protocols running JavaScript, Flash, or Active-X plugins can compromise your computer, which is why you need anti-malware software as well or use a more secure browser. There is a long running debate about browser security, which has yet to be resolved. In 2011 a study found that Google Chrome was the most secure browser, but by 2013 a user poll suggested that Mozilla Firefox was superior. I use Google Chrome and Mozilla Firefox, and have actually disabled Microsoft Internet Explorer, as in my opinion it is insecure when compared to other browsers.

These simple technological fixes will make you a little safer on the web, but they only scratch the surface of cyber threat. There are other methods of cyber attack such as spam and phishing, but these are social cyber threats and not technological cyber-threats. There are no "firewall" or "anti-malware" software upgrades for the human brain – yet!

Corporate Cyber Threat

Corporate cyber-threat takes threat levels to a whole new dimension. Problems with data protection and data privacy sit side by side with the problems of data integrity and data security. The legal requirements of data protection, the needs for businesses to compartmentalize data and the ongoing ability to use computers in the day-to-day running of the business take precedence over everything.

There are regulations about the protection of customer databases and financial data, regulations about credit card number storage and regulations about accounting procedures, audits and possible insider trading. Every business is legally required to uphold all of these standards. None of them protect your business and it is up to you to protect your data and your computer.

This is where the CIA principle, also known as the CIA triad comes in useful for evaluating IT business strategies. If you follow the three basic tenets of the CIA principle, your business has a better chance of surviving and thriving.

Confidentiality

Your business data means nothing if anyone can steal it – your business plans, financial projections, project plans and even industrial secrets are all vulnerable to data theft. Allowing unrestricted access to your business data is like leaving the key under the mat of your back door! Make sure you have a proper password protected access scheme that allows full logging of all usage of your systems. Not everyone should have access to every bit of data on the system; only if they need it for their work. If you value your data, make sure you use properly configured access control lists to control everyone who can read or copy your data. If you don't understand this, then hire someone who does – before one of your employees steals your client list and becomes your competitor.

Integrity

Your business data means nothing to you if it is incomplete, corrupted or modified without proper permission. In my experience as a corporate IT manager, I have found that a very large percentage of alleged computer errors are actually either finger problems caused by human operators or data problems caused by incomplete, inconsistent or badly programmed systems. Genuine computer problems are very rare. Databases that are inconsistent are useless. You need to sweep through and clean up your databases on a regular basis to clean up duplicated entries and fill in the blanks. If you use multiple databases, you need to maintain the integrity of one against the other. There is no point in having multiple databases across different computers if they do not hold the same data – this leads to duplication of effort and possible customer dissatisfaction.

Accessibility

Evidence from the US National Archives & Records Administration shows that 93 per cent of all businesses that lose their data for 10 days or more filed for bankruptcy within a year, and that 50 per cent of companies affected in this way filed for bankruptcy immediately. Maintaining access to your business data in times of crisis is very important and should be part of any disaster recovery program. Depending on the turnover of your data, you should have backups. You do have backups, don't you? If not you are likely to be one of the 93 per cent I just mentioned. Backup early. Backup often. If you value your business data, then you must backup daily, weekly, monthly and annually. Store the backups in a fireproof safe. Make copies of your important backups and store them offsite in another fireproof safe somewhere else. Hopefully you will never need them, but those backups are peace of mind when fires, floods, or earthquakes wipe out your main office – they will allow you to continue your business when your ill-prepared competitors have ceased to trade.

Why is the Computer Security Industry Failing Us?

Or rather: How easy is it to protect yourself from your computer's vulnerabilities?

Modern computer security mythology runs in stages, but at every step of the sales pitch the message is the same: the only way to be safe is to buy more (and better) computer security services and software. How realistic is this? In this modern age of cyber threat, when the typical methods of cyber attack are zero day vulnerabilities inside nearly all of the global computer population, there is no 100 per cent surefire method of securing your computer. Many computer security products are nothing more than digital snake oil – promising the world but delivering only the placebo of apparent security. The current computer security industry uses a three-step process to sell their products, but do they make us safer?

PROBLEM Your computer is under threat. Doing nothing is not an option. You must take proactive measures to guarantee the security of your computer.

THREAT You should take various measures to protect your computer because the possibility of your computer being compromised is high. Take steps to secure your computer and the information contained on it before cyber-criminals take control of it and steal all your money and data.

SOLUTION Buy "Brand X" security solution from the ACME Corporation to protect your computer.

The fundamental message is this: If you do nothing about the security of your computer it will be subject to hostile takeover, become owned by a botnet herder, and then used to send spam, or as a cyber weapon against other computers.

This part is truth at least, but there is no 100 per cent guarantee of computer security. Computer security software can only prevent known security problems. With the current state of the art in malware using zero day vulnerabilities, it doesn't matter what you spend on computer security because it will not make you safer!

If we analyze the standard attack vectors behind 90 per cent of computer intrusions on the internet, we find that the most dangerous attacks are the least expected. The huge growth in client-side attacks on browsers and plugins allow for instant compromise and downloading of malware. The reactive role of current computer security software means that *nobody* is safe.

The commonest methods of current computer exploitation are described below. It can be seen that there is no chance that any current combination of anti-malware packages can prevent infection within the context of zero day vulnerabilities and the sophistication of modern malware. Modern approaches to internet security, which use the "white list" approach – i.e. allow only connections with known, trusted websites – are also doomed to fail. Let's begin by connecting to a website – there are two possibilities.

Possibility One

The victim is directed to a server hosting malware. Cross-site scripting attacks that fake website URLs, phishing emails, links in social networking or blogging sites and fake URLs embedded in spam are all used.

Possibility Two

The victim is directed to a black listed server hosting malware. Cross-site scripting attacks that fake website URLs, phishing emails, links in social networking or blogging sites and fake URLs embedded in spam are all used to lure unsuspecting victims to malware sites. If the website is black listed, the the user will be prevented from accessing the site and there will be no infection.

A black listed server will always be automatically rejected or a popup will allow the user to decide to allow access. The default deny status of that website is the first level of protection against malware hosting websites.

A white listed server will be automatically allowed to connect to your computer, the incoming connections will then be passed to other stages in the computer security process – your firewall and anti-malware software.

Always denying possible malware hosting websites to connect to your computer is a good idea. If your blacklist software is up to date, then it will always flag up known problems with known malware hosting domains, IP addresses and websites.

It is the steps following the "allow" option of white listed sites that is interesting. Here the door is opened to a possible cyber threat from otherwise innocent, but compromised, internet servers. Any internet server that appears on the white list will automatically be allowed to communicate with the victim computer even if it has been compromised and contains malware.

So the website server has been compromised and now the malware can exploit your computer. This is when you find out how good your computer security is. How good is your anti-virus, anti-malware, or code-execution protection software? How often is your computer and computer security software updated? How much protection does it really give?

The truth is, none of these factors guarantee protection. You can be exploited by a zero day vulnerability cyber attack even if you have the biggest and best computer security software there is. Nation states and large corporations have been compromised by zero day exploits, and if they spend billions of dollars every year on cyber security how can the average user protect themselves using consumer grade cyber-security software?

There is *no* protection against zero day attacks. It was estimated that fixing the exploits in a recent upgrade to a commercial cyber attack crime-ware package – and the subsequent time taken to issue software patches to ensure system security – took Microsoft seven weeks. This is why there is a huge underground black market for computer vulnerabilities – a digital black market that trades on computer insecurity.

Why can't the software industry get it right? For years computer security experts and hackers have been pointing out flaws in software, but these never seem to get properly fixed. Each new release of an operating system will contain a new set of vulnerabilities. Each updated version of a browser or plugin will contain a new set of vulnerabilities. Patching makes things worse – it allows dark-side hackers to reverse-engineer the patch and write a new exploit. The level of cyber threat is so high that it no longer exists only in your computer or smart phone. In this modern age of cyber threat, smart homes, cars, fridges and even insulin pumps and pacemakers can be hacked.

For this reason, I have lost my faith in the idea of computers as a force for positive change in society. I have lost my faith in the idea of the internet as a force for positive change in society. I no longer believe that the World Wide Web is a wonderful invention because it has become an agent for the perpetual surveillance society. We should be living in a brave new world of instant communication; instead we live in an information dystopia where social networking is more important than using computers to build a better society. I have gone from being a tech-geek who promoted the use of computers and the internet to a digital apostate who has rejected the current paradigm.

But most of all I no longer believe that computer security is possible. Despite all the attempts – and the growth of a hugely profitable computer security industry – we are no safer than we were twenty years ago. On the contrary, the computer security industry makes us less safe. They sell the illusion that if we install Brand-X firewall and Brand-Z anti-virus software we will be safe.

The sad truth is that new malware is rarely spotted by existing anti-virus software – it needs to be captured, analyzed and reverse engineered – and only then can a new anti-virus signature can be added to the database. Zero day vulnerabilities using drive-by infection cannot be stopped by a firewall – all the vulnerabilities are inside the browser or add-ons. The sad truth is that nobody is safe in cyberspace. If we choose to live in the world of ubiquitous networking and communication – where every connected device represents a vector of cyber attack – then we need to adjust our thinking and learn to live with the constant background of cyber threat.

20

INFORMATION DYSTOPIA

We are living in the age of the internet, the age of instant communication. We are living in the best of times – and the worst of times though nobody knows it. The potential of the internet to facilitate communication has grown so fast that our minds cannot keep up with it. Email allows us to keep in touch with loved ones, while social networks allow us to spread trivial ideas to potentially thousands of people at the speed of light.

In the last ten years the number of people connected to the internet has grown by 528 per cent. There are over 644 million websites on the internet and possibly over a trillion web pages – but that is the tip of the iceberg. The "Deep Web" – sites inaccessible to search engines – is estimated to be 400–550 times larger than the indexed web. It seems that the expansion of the world wide web follows **Moore's Law** and that doubles every 18-24 months. This means at the current rate of expansion there will be approximately two billion websites by 2015. We take computational devices for granted – they run our lives. We trust our computers to organize our lives and track our appointments. We use our smartphones to instantly connect with anyone on the planet. Yet the information we share is available to almost everyone who wants it. We have elected to live in a world where everything we do – from what we eat for breakfast to the current book we are reading – is semi-public knowledge. We have chosen to live in a digital panopticon where we are never sure if we are watched or not, where we validate our existence through the number of followers we have on Twitter and other social networking sites. Indeed, if we feel we are not being watched, we worry about our online status even more.

The age of cyberspace should be an age of reason where we can communicate with anyone at any moment, look up entries in an online encyclopedia, or search for anything via the numerous search engines available on the web. We have access to more information in the digital age than ever before. The Royal Library of Alexandria did not hold as much information as cyberspace. The collective libraries of London, New York and Washington do not hold as much information as cyberspace. No library in the world holds as much information as cyber space. Our lives have become digitized without us realizing it.

Digital information is not like written information. It is mutable, changeable, flexible and capable of being abused. Digital information is infinitely replicable and each copy has the potential to be an identical copy while leaving the original information intact.

The internet itself is nothing more than information. The computer protocols that allow us to connect to the internet and access websites are nothing more than computer code, which is another form of information. This strange confluence of ideas – code and data – is what holds the internet together. What happens when the data is stolen or the code is modified?

The results are apparent. The internet should have heralded a new golden age of communication. Instead we are living in a new dark age of information hell. The potential power of the internet to enhance our civilization has been subverted and we live in a new age of cyber threat where computers have become the enemy. We can no longer trust our computers, and as we have seen in this book all of the following cyber threats are the enemy.

Threat One: Cybercrime

Even if you don't have a credit card or use online banking, cybercrime is a major threat. The use of hardened malware by cyber-criminals for illegal purposes is well-known. Even if you not infected by a banking trojan such as Zeus, the vast amount of RATs available on the internet place everybody at risk. There is no solution for this problem. The current market for zero day exploits guarantees that somebody somewhere can make money by exploiting the vulnerabilities inside your computer. Once your computer has been compromised by a RAT or a botnet client your computer can be used to perpetrate more internet crimes. If your computer is not properly secured, it becomes part of the problem. Secure your computer now and become part of the solution. Local computer security is also global computer security. Denying cyber-criminals the low-hanging fruit of unsecured computers helps to degrade their operations. Securing your computer against RAT or botnet infection not only helps you, it helps everybody on the internet.

Threat Two: Cyber-terror

Is cyber-terrorism a real threat? The evidence shows that cyber-terrorists use the internet in the same was as everybody else – to communicate and spread their memes through cyberspace. There is a fine line between the cyber-hacktivists and cyber-terrorists – both act from a political motivation – but the difference is apparent when projected into the real world. It is unlikely that cyber-hacktivists such as Anonymous or LulzSec will resort to violence to achieve their aims, but the cyber-terrorists want nothing more than violence. However, the apparent similarities between cyber-terrorists and cyber-activists should not be ignored. There is a cross over between hacktivists and other cyber groups which the USA has started to explore, claiming that links between Anonymous and terrorist hackers amount to conspiracy. If this can be shown – and certainly the Anonymous and LulzSec groups conspired online – then prosecutions can be made under the Racketeer Influenced and Corrupt Organizations Act (RICO) laws normally used against organized crime.

Threat Three: Cyberwar

A few years ago cyberwar was pure science fiction. Now we know that cyberwar is real. The 2013 Snowden allegations that the USA were responsible for the design, manufacture and release of the Stuxnet worm against the Iranian nuclear development project changed everything forever. A new arms race – for digital weapons – is now inevitable. The growth of the black market for zero day vulnerabilities demonstrates this. Once upon a time, only black software laboratories bought zero day vulnerabilities. Now nation state actors are allegedly purchasing those same vulnerabilities for up to ten times their value on the cybercrime market. Nation state actors have their digital cadres who roam the internet seeking and downloading malware. Once the malware has been found, it is easy to decompile and recycle the techniques contained inside the software. Now the source code for the Stuxnet worm is available to any cyber-terrorist or cyber warrior for modification. Cyber weapons have arrived and they have changed the threat landscape forever.

Threat Four: Cyber-paranoia

Nobody knows the true depth of the secret governmental programs used against criminals and terrorists but the true damage is caused by the assumption that everybody is a potential suspect. The growth of social networks allows governments to track our social activities in real time. Modern smart phones are nothing more than advanced surveillance and tracking devices. Our emails are monitored, our banking transactions are tracked and our licence plates recorded on a myriad of CCTV cameras. But what does all of this mean for the internet itself?

The trend is not just in the familiar attacks on the technical infrastructure of the internet which gain so much press, but the attacks that undermine the utility of services offered over the internet. These services are the "killer applications" that almost everyone uses and takes for granted. These threats undermine the confidence, and thus the growth and the use of services such as email, e-commerce, social networking and online banking. Cyber threat is a threat because people perceive it to be a threat.

If there was no cyber threat then the online economy could grow much larger than it already is, adding billions or possibly trillions to the global economy. Cyberspace might not be a "real" place but the interaction between cyberspace and the real world is important for all of us.

Where is your money when you go to an ATM? Inside the bank? Inside the ATM? Or somewhere less tangible – the space between the spaces. If cyberspace – or even part of cyberspace – is destroyed and your financial records are no longer available, where is your money then?

These cyber threats undermine the utility of computers, networks and even the internet itself as a means of communication. Computer users have to worry about security and use firewalls, anti-virus, anti-spyware, anti-adware and anti-rootkit software. How long before the crushing burden of purchasing, installing and maintaining large amounts of security software becomes too much for ordinary users? Will they just give up and not bother connecting to the internet? Already statistics suggest that between 15 and 38 per cent of internet users refuse to use online financial services because they do not trust them. Reducing cyber threat across the board will build confidence in those users, allowing a rapid growth of online economy.

Internet infrastructure is built with multiple redundancy and multiple pathways designed to re-route communication around damaged portions. But electronic infrastructure attacks, traffic spikes and storms caused by malware can cripple parts of the internet, causing degraded connectivity in other parts of the net as traffic is re-routed through other pathways. Although the internet was built to be fault-tolerant and route around problems, the constant damage caused by botnets, hackers, hacktivists and cyber-warriors is beginning to take its toll. This all undermines the utility of the internet as a reliable means of communication.

Could the Internet Die?

It is very unlikely that any major vector of cyber attack will kill the internet itself, because without the internet most cyber attacks become impossible. Internet hacktivists, cyber-criminals, cyber-terrorists and cyber-warriors rely on the internet to wage their cyberwars. Knocking down a website with DDoS attacks does not affect the web itself – just the website. It has been suggested that Anonymous called off their DDoS attack on PayPal because the majority of the Anonymous collective relied on PayPal as an online service provider.

But this does not mean that the internet would not be affected in times of crisis. As the 2008 cyberwar between Russia and Georgia highlights, internet attacks are a very useful force multiplier within conventional conflicts. For non-nation state actors – such as cyber-terrorists – the option of physical destruction of internet infrastructure is a powerful force multiplier. A single **back hoe** attack on key internet choke points, or a car bomb beside a large internet provider, will always cause more damage than a cyber attack.

If cyberspace – or even part of cyber space – is destroyed and the ATM no longer works and credit card transactions are no longer possible, where is your money?

War has always implied physical threat and if an open "shooting war" broke out, maintaining our status on social networking groups would be the least of our worries. Let's consider an attack on the "global village" fostered by the internet. People communicate daily through chat, email and social networking sites in a transnational manner, building new virtual communities. What happens when the digital global village is caught in a digital airstrike and destroyed even if only as digital collateral damage? The potential of cyber warfare to destroy the internet is a real and present danger. Incorrectly used cyber weapons could run out of control, wiping out data and destroying computers across the world. Already there are viral techniques that can wipe out the Basic Input/Output System (BIOS) of your computer – turning into an expensive door-stop. The same viral techniques can be used against cell phones – making them as useful as a brick for communications purposes. The only protection is to use a fully "air gapped" network – one that does not allow access to the internet. But even this is not 100 per cent safe, as viruses or worms could be introduced through floppy disks or USB memory sticks. Old-fashioned vectors of attack – such as boot-block viruses – can be used on USB memory or other memory cards. If you find a memory stick somewhere, make sure it hasn't been left around as viral bait – a method of subverting your computer and maybe every computer inside your organization.

Yet the idea of the internet is now heavily embedded in public consciousness. People take the internet – and the devices attached to it – for granted. In order to minimize cyber threats, the ordinary user needs to be educated in the nature of the threat and how to take proactive measures accordingly. We can only stem cyber threat if we also stem the growth in the potential attack surface represented by millions of ordinary users who have no technical skills. The average internet user buys a computer, takes it home and plugs it into the internet without ever thinking about the impact that unsecured computer has on everybody. All users should be taught to secure their computers from the very first moment they attach it to the internet. Once ordinary users make a commitment to local system security, it not only benefits them, but every other internet user also.

We are living in the age of the internet – and cyber threat is inside the system. The cyber attack vectors that could compromise our computers are everywhere and no website can be trusted. Our computers are potential cyber weapons and the internet itself is a potential cyber weapon. Yet the internet continues to flourish. We need to become accustomed to cyber threats – to evaluate the risk – and take steps to minimize that risk. We need to seek out and prosecute cyber-criminals and cyber-terrorists who use the internet for transnational criminal activities. We need to become proactive in system security instead of being reactive. The current models of computer security are broken or flawed – and until we fix the way we think about internet security – cyber threat will always be with us.

GLOSSARY

Advanced Persistent Threat (APT): An advanced persistent threat that targets a company or group over a long period of time, installing trojans and spyware and exfiltrating private and confidential documents. A typical APT is much more dangerous than the cyber-threat possibilities of cyber-hacktivists and cyber-terrorists and are often suspected to be the work of nation state actors involved in cyber espionage.

Adware: A form of *malware* which serves up unwanted advertising onto a computer and which can sometimes redirect your browser to another website based on your current activities.

Anonymous: A loose collective of *cyber-hacktivists* considered by some to be actually *cyber-terrorists*. Like many of their fellow *cyber hacktivists*, Anonymous take great delight in digital *détournement* and digital *schadenfreude*.

Astro Turfing: The use of multiple *sock puppets* to affect public opinion in the *fifth domain* by pretending to be "grass roots" opinion.

Asymmetrical Conflict: Any form of conflict where a smaller group attacks a larger group. A modern example of this would be the current conflict between the United Sataes and their allies against radical Jihadi Islamic groups such as Al-Qaeda.

Back Hoe/JCB Attack: The use of a back hoe in the USA, or the type of mechanical digger commonly called "JCB" in the UK, to directly attack physical internet infrastructure such as fibre optic cables. In 2003 a Ph.D candidate, Sean P Gorman, calculated the internet choke points across the USA and concluded that physical attacks would disrupt the internet more efficiently than cyber attacks.

BIOS (Basic Input Output System): The BIOS of a computer is the most basic part of the software system which is responsible for writing to a screen, accepting keyboard input and reading files from hard drives or floppy disks.

Battle Space: Traditionally the battle space was the domains of warfare such as land, sea, air and outer space, but the arrival of the internet has led to the formation of new military units, indicating that *cyberspace* is the *fifth domain* of modern warfare.

Black Hat Hacker: A skilled computer user who understands computers and system security, but who uses that knowledge to cause *internet mayhem* and *cybercrime*. Not to be confused with *white hat hackers*.

Botnet: A large number of computers that have been compromised using a *vulnerability*. Once compromised, the *zombie* computers can be controlled from a command and control centre and be used for sending *SPAM*, *distributed denial of service* attacks, hosting of illegal material and general *internet mayhem*.

Botnet Herder: The cyber criminal who compromised the *zombie* computers and now can control thousands, or hundreds of thousands, of computers to cause *internet mayhem*.

Boundless Informant: Alleged *NSA* software that accesses telephone *metadata* for future analysis using *traffic analysis*, but which is targeted against countries most likely to host potential radical Jihadi Islamic terrorists.

Bullet Proof Hosting: A form of website hosting that guarantees the *cyber criminal* the website will not be removed even when law enforcement officials request it. Used for *malware* hosting sites, *phishing* sites, and illegal content such as child pornography.

Computer Security: An oxymoron, but one that is highly profitable for a large number of companies, which have assured us that their products protect us, but have been unable to prevent *internet mayhem*.

Counter Intelligence Program (COINTELPRO): A method used by law enforcement agencies to combat alleged communists who were part of the 'enemy within'. At the height of the Cold War organizations such as the 'Black Panthers' and 'Students for a Democratic Society' were all penetrated by *sock puppets* and informants who acted as trolls to destroy the movement from within.

Crimeware: Any piece of *malware* which is designed to facilitate *cybercrime,* such as *phishing* kits, *exploit* kits, *botnet* clients, *remote access trojans* and tools for generating custom *malware* such as *worms.* Crimeware is mostly sold on the digital underground, but "open source" crimeware is also available on the internet.

Cyber-activists: Normal political activists who use the internet to promote their agenda or cause, and to organize grass roots activists and sometimes even demonstrations, but who do not break the law in their use of the internet. Not to be confused with *cyber hacktivists* or *cyber-terrorists.*

Cyber Attack: Anything that contributes to *internet mayhem* damages *cyber space* and leads to the formation of an *information dystopia* and a *perpetual surveillance society.*

Cybercrime: The use of *cyber space* by transnational criminal organizations whose sole motivation in using hacking techniques is theft of data and money.

Cyber-criminals: Loosely organized criminals who use the internet as a means of communication, a market place for stolen user credentials, and a method of organizing large digital heists worth millions of dollars.

Cyber-hacktivists: Loose knit groups of *black hat hackers* who use hacking techniques to illegally access computers, organize distributed *denial of service attacks* and steal data for publication on the internet so that everyone may see. Not to be confused with *cyber-activists* or *cyber-terrorists.*

Cyberspace: The sum total of everything that is digitally connected on our planet by the phone system and the internet.

Cyber-terrorists: Normal terrorists who use the internet to spread propaganda, gather intelligence and possibly plan attacks. Cyber-terrorists also use *black hat* hacking techniques for breaking into servers to use as storage, deface web servers and mount *denial of service* attacks. Not to be confused with *cyber-activists* or *cyber-hacktivists* because cyber-terrorists always have the possibility of using extreme violence.

Cyber-warriors: Nation state-backed security experts who use *black hat* hacking techniques to perform espionage and possibly cyber attacks using *cyber weapons*. As they have the official backing of their governments, they are far more dangerous than *cyber-hacktivists* and *cyber-terrorists* because they cannot be caught and prosecuted.

Cyber Weapon: A device or a piece of software that is designed to act as a *force multiplier* in a conventional conflict by damaging computer systems, programs, networks, data and *SCADA* systems.

Data Mining: The use of large databases, or multiple databases, to look for patterns in behaviour. While data mining can be useful in fighting *cybercrime* or determining consumer preferences, there is no evidence that using data mining to fight the "war on terror" makes us safer. In fact the use of data mining against terrorists is adding to *internet mayhem* and could lead to an *information dystopia*.

Denial of Service (DoS): A denial of service attack overloads a server or website with so much data that it becomes unstable, unreliable or possibly even crashes.

Détournement: A French word that describes the technique originating from the "Situationist International" movement, and which recycles advertising and marketing techniques to make the contradiction of the original message manifest. Modern *cyber-hacktivists* such as *Anonymous* and *LulzSec* use digital détournement to steal data, publish it, reduce the value of the data to nothing and then enjoy the resulting *schadenfreude*, contributing to a higher level of *internet mayhem*.

Distributed Denial of Service (DDoS): The use of multiple attack vectors using a *denial of service* attack simultaneously. These attacks can be coordinated across the internet using IRC – as in the case of the distributed denial of service attacks by *Anonymous* – or more commonly by using a *botnet* of compromised computers.

Drive By Infection: A *black hat* hacking technique which *exploits* a *vulnerability* in the victim's computer to download and install *malware*. *Drive by infection* is used by *cyber criminals, cyber-hacktivists, cyber-terrorists* and *cyber warriors*.

Echelon: A not-so-secret *SIGINT* program, which was designed to intercept and store all voice and data communications by satellite. Now superceded by *GCHQ* operations such as *Tempora*.

Exploit: A program or technical procedure that allows a *cyber criminal* to use a *vulnerability* to compromise a computer for whatever reason.

Exploit Kit: A piece of *crimeware* designed to facilitate *drive by infection* by packaging together a number of *exploits* which are then placed on a website. Traditional techniques such as *phishing* and social networking are then used to lure the victim to the website, who is duly infected by *malware* such as a *remote access trojan*.

Fifth Domain: (i) The four domains of advertising and marketing were billboards, press, radio and television, but now *cyberspace* is the fifth domain. (ii) The four domains of the *battle space* were land, sea, air and outer space, but now *cyberspace* is the fifth domain.

Force Multiplier: Any technique which, in an *asymmetrical conflict* allows the smaller force to have a significant advantage over a larger force. In conventional warfare a force multiplier is any technique that supports military operations across the entire *battle space* to gain a miltary or political advantage.

GCHQ: The "Government Communications Headquarters" is the UK equivalent of the *NSA* and heavily involved in *SIGINT* and possibly the development of *cyber weapons*. GCHQ is alleged to be a part of the *Tempora* project which taps into the global fibre optic network, and also shares this information with the *NSA*.

Grey Hat Hacker: A skilled computer user who understands computers and system security but is both a *black hat hacker* and a *white hat hacker* at the same time.

Hacker: A skilled computer user who understands computers, networks and system security. Hackers built the internet and the world wide web. Not to be confused with *black hat hackers*.

Honeypot: A computer whose only value is in being compromised by a third party. A typical honeypot looks like a ripe target to a *black hat hacker*, but in reality is a tethered goat designed to lure the evildoer into a place where their methods can be studied in detail.

Information Dystopia: The current state of *internet mayhem* which is leading us into an situation where the internet is the weapon of choice for *cyber criminals*, *cyber hacktivists*, *cyber-terrorists* and *cyber-warriors*. When combined with the use of *cyberspace* as the perfect technology for enabling a *perpetual surveillance society*, we end up with an *information dystopia* in which the value of *cyberspace* as a means of communication is devalued to almost nothing, as the threat of cyber attack far outways the risk of using the internet.

Internet: A weapon of mass distraction and the sole vector for *internet mayhem*. If the current situation of *internet mayhem* is not addressed soon, it will allow the formation of an *information dystopia*.

Internet Mayhem: The ongoing process of devaluing *cyberspace* to zero by *cyber-criminals, cyber-hacktivists, cyber-terrorists, cyber-warriors* and the use of the internet as a tool for ensuring a *perpetual surveillance society.* The current trends lead to state of *information dystopia* where the invention of the internet and the world wide web represent a huge threat to modern society and democracy.

JCB see **Back Hoe Attack**

Koobface: A group of cyber criminals who caused *internet mayhem* by using social networking websites to install *malware* such as *adware* and *spyware* onto vulnerable computers. By using *pay per install* techniques the Koobface gang raked in an estimated $2 million.

Lab 1313: The possible home of a Russian cyberwar facility similar to *Unit 61398* in China and *Unit 8200* in Israel. Allegedly involved in the active development of *cyber weapons.*

LulzSec: Alleged offshoot of *Anonymous,* who were tracked down and arrested after hacking their way across the planet and stealing huge amounts of confidential data and publishing it on the web.

Malware: A piece of software which has been written with evil intent and designed to cause *internet mayhem.* Common forms of malware are *adware, spyware, remote access trojans, worms* and *viruses.*

Man in the middle attack: A phrase from cryptography describing a situation where a cyber-criminal gets between two computers so that all information passed between those two computers is available for reading. The messages intended for the genuine website are passed to the cyber-criminal, who then passes them onto the website. In the other direction, information sent from the genuine websites is passed through the man in the middle before being passed back to the victim. The Zeus banking Trojan uses this type of attack.

Moore's Law In 1965 Intel co-founder Gordon E. Moore made an interesting observation about the exponential nature of technological growth, and noted that the number of transistors on integrated circuits doubles approximately every two years. We now know that "Moore's Law" has much wider applications and, can for example, predict the vast growth of the internet and the web.

New Cold War: The current situation which is causing *internet mayhem* as the USA, Russia and China use the internet for digital espionage, *maskirovka* and low level cyber warfare.

MAINWAY: Alleged NSA database that stores *metadata* such as phone billing records for the entire USA.

MARINA: Alleged NSA database which stores internet *metadata* for an estimated 86% of all internet traffic which crosses US controlled internet connections.

Maskirovka: The Russian word for 'deception', which was used in the cold war and now appears to be applicable to what some commentators have called the *new cold war*.

Metadata: The raw communitions data used in *traffic analysis* which does not access the content of the message, but records the sender, recipient, time, date, call duration and possibly location.

NSA: The US 'National Security Agency', which collects *SIGINT* and is possibly involved in the design and building of cyber weapons such as *Stuxnet*.

Nucleon: Alleged *NSA* database that collects the contents of telephone calls for future analysis and *data mining*.

Panopticon: Designed by the English philosopher Jeremy Bentham, the panopticon was intended to be the perfect prison where every inmate could be watched at any time, but nobody knew when they were being watched.

Pay Per Install: A technique used by ruthless and very dubious *black hat hackers* and *cyber criminals* to encourage other *cyber criminals* to install a*dware, spyware* and *remote access trojans* onto victim's computers. Although typical pay per install prices are low, from a few cents to a few dollars, the use of these methods can net *cyber criminals* big bucks.

Perpetual Surveillance Society: Our modern world where everything that we do, both in *cyberspace* and the real world is recorded on a computer somewhere, allowing for *data mining* techniques and ensuring that we are all the 'enemy within' in the context of the current 'war on terror'.

Phishing: The use of *SPAM* to lure an unsuspecting victim into visiting a website that is either a fake site which looks like a real online banking website, or a website hosting malware allowing for *drive by infection.*

PRISM: Alleged *NSA* program that uses a variety of collection techniques to build huge data bases of behaviour in *cyberspace* with the sole purpose of *data mining* and searching for possible terrorist activity.

Project Avatar: An alleged *NSA* project that could be internet rumour, reality, or digital *maskirovka.* The Avatar Project is designed to build a profile of everybody who uses *cyberspace* using *SIGINT* data collection across the whole of *cyberspace* for use in intelligence gathering, *traffic analysis* and *data mining*.

Remote Access Trojan (RAT): A piece of *malware* designed to allow access to a compromised computer. RATs typically allow monitoring of keystrokes, screen activity, microphones and cameras. More sophisticated RATs such as *Zeus* allow the theft of user credentials and banking theft.

SCADA: 'Supervisory Control and Data Acquisition'. The combination of hardware and software that controls power stations, water and sewage pumping stations, nuclear plants and much more. SCADA controls the infrastructure which makes our lives easy and thus is an easy target for *cyberwar.*

Shadenfreude: The German word which means "taking a delight in the misfortunes of others". When *cyber hacktivists* such as *Anonymous* and *LulzSec* use digital *schadenfreude,* they delight in the level of *internet mayhem* they cause.

SIGNIT: An acronym for "Signals Intelligence", which is nothing more than the collection and storage of communications data flowing through radio, satellites, undersea cables and the internet for later analysis, possible decryption and *data mining.*

Skimmer: A device fitted to the front of an ATM, which allows a *cyber criminal* to steal the data on the magnetic stripe of the card, along with the PIN to access that card. This is then used to make duplicate cards in order to steal money from the victim.

Sock Puppet: A fake internet user with a hidden agenda, who pretends to be one person while actually being another and promotes advertising, marketing, propaganda or disinformation.

SPAM: Unsolicited email that is sent in bulk to huge numbers of recipients across the internet and which normally advertises prescription drugs, sexual services and dodgy websites.

Spyware: This is *malware* that tracks the victim's online activity and sends the information to a *black hat hacker.* While typically used in conjuction with *adware* back in the early days of the internet, spyware has now largely been superceded by *remote access trojans,* which are more efficient and can steal more informaton.

Sting Board: A fake website that is owned by law enforcement or intelligence agencies designed to attract *cyber criminals* and *cyber-terrorists* and gather intelligence and evidence in order to infiltrate and destroy their organizations.

Stuxnet: A *worm* that has been called the first *cyber weapon.* Allegedly created by the USA and Israel, this *cyber weapon* damaged the Iranian nuclear program.

Tempora: Alleged *SIGINT* operation by *GCHQ*, which taps into over 200 fibre optic cables in the UK. Evidence suggests that all data is shared with the *NSA*, allowing US intelligence agencies to access data about US citizens without legal oversight.

Traffic Analysis: The use of raw *SIGINT* data to determine who sent what to whom and when. Using traffic analysis allows the further analysis of networked of possible *cyber criminals* and *cyber-terrorists*, but the collection of this data could led to the violation of the expectation of privacy across the internet.

Unit 8200: The possible home of an Israeli *cyberwar* facility similar to *Unit 61398* in China and *Lab 1313* in Russia. Alleged to have helped to create the *stuxnet worm.*

Unit 61398: The possible home of a Chinese *cyberwar* facility similar to *Unit 1313* in Russia and *Unit 8200* in Israel. Allegedly responsible for a large number of cyber espionage incidents.

Victim: Possibly anyone who uses cyberspace for any reason, as the current security model is so comprehensibly broken that *computer security* cannot be guaranteed.

Virus: A piece of *malware* that uses a variety of infection methods to replicate across computers, such as floppy disks, memory sticks and infected software. Not to be confused with a *worm.*

Vulnerability: Any method of gaining illegal access to a computer. These can include infected documents, *drive by infection* and the use of default or stolen passwords.

White Hat Hacker: A skilled computer user who understands computers and system security, but who uses that knowledge to try and stop *internet mayhem* and *cybercrime.* Not to be confused with *grey hat hackers* or *black hat hackers.*

WHOIS: An internet wide database that contains information on internet hosts and domains. Making a search on the WHOIS database should reveal the true owner of an internet host. Although it is illegal in some countries to falsify WHOIS information, cyber-criminals abuse the system on a regular basis.

Worm: A piece of *malware* which uses the internet as the primary method of spreading by infecting vulnerable hosts and then searching for more computers to infect. Not to be confused with a *virus,* even though some worms use viral spreading techniques.

Xkeyscore: Alleged *NSA* program that allows a security analyst to monitor internet communications in real time, while allowing *data mining* using the databases from the *PRISM* project.

Zeus: A *remote access trojan* that redirects online banking operations through a server under the control of a *cyber-criminal* and steals money from the victim's account while feeding false information to the victim's computer.

Zero Day: A computer *vulnerability* that has not yet been patched and which presents a serious security risk.

Zombie: A computer that has been compromised using a *vulnerability* and which now runs a *remote access trojan* as a *botnet* client.

BIBLIOGRAPHY

BOOKS

Glenny, Misha. *McMafia: A Journey Through the Global Criminal Underworld*, Vintage, 2008

Greenberg, Andy. *This Machine Kills Secrets: Julian Assange, the Cypherpunks, and Their Fight to Empower Whistleblowers*, Plume, 2012

Henderson, Scott J. Dark *Visitor: Inside the World of the Chinese Hackers*, Lulu, 2007

Poulson, Kevin. *Kingpin: How One Hacker Took Over the Billion-Dollar Cybercrime Underground*, Crown, 2011

Sterling, Bruce. *The Hacker Crackdown: Law & Disorder on the Electronic Frontier*, Bantam Books, 1992

Watts, Duncan J. *Everything Is Obvious Once You Know The Answer: How Common Sense Fails*, Atlantic Books, 2012

WEB REFERENCES

Anderson, Ross & Barton, Chris & Böhme, Rainer & Clayton, Richard & van Eeten, Michel J.G. & Michael, Levi & Moore, Tyler & Savage, Stefan. "Measuring the Cost of Cybercrime", 2012
http://weis2012.econinfosec.org/papers/Anderson_WEIS2012.pdf

Ashford, Warwick. "UK and US Collaborating on Cyber Weapons, says Snowden", *Computer Weekly*, 2013
http://www.computerweekly.com/news/2240202997/UK-and-US-collaborating-on-cyber-weapons-says-Snowden

BBC. "UK to create new cyber defense force", 2013
http://www.bbc.co.uk/news/uk-24321717

Brenner, Susan W. "Organized Cybercrime? How Cyberspace May Affect the Structure of Criminal Relations", North Carolina Journal of Law & Technology Volume 4, Issue 1, 2002
http://www.ncjolt.org/sites/default/files/brenner_.pdf

Bogdan, Popa. "100,000 New Phishing Websites Every Week", Softpedia, 2007
http://news.softpedia.com/news/100-000-New-Phishing-Websites-Every-Week-58057.shtml

Boston Consulting Group. "The Connected World: The Internet Economy in the G–20: The $4.2 Trillion Opportunity", 2012
http://www.bcg.com/documents/file100409.pdf

Bump, Phillip. "Update: Now We Know Why Googling 'Pressure Cookers' Gets a Visit from Cops", The Wire, 2013
http://www.thewire.com/national/2013/08/government-knocking-doors-because-google-searches/67864/

Carr, Jeffrey. "28 Nation States With Cyber Warfare Capabilities", Digital Dao weblog, 2011
http://jeffreycarr.blogspot.co.uk/2011/09/27-nation-states-with-cyber warfare.html

Rafati, Mohammed (Siavash)."Iranian Cyber Warfare Threat Assessment", Cyberwarzone, 2010
http://cyberwarzone.com/content/iranian-cyber-warfare-threat-assessment

Daily Telegraph, "Russia: A Gangster State", 2012
http://www.telegraph.co.uk/news/worldnews/europe/russia/9107811/Russia-a-gangster-state.html
Deloitte report, "Cybercrime: A Clear and Present Danger", 2010
http://www.deloitte.com/assets/dcomunitedstates/local%20assets/documents/aers/us_aers_deloitte%20cyber%20crime%20pov%20jan252010.pdf

Deputy Secretary of Defense Memorandum. "Subject: The Definition of Cyberspace", 2008
http://www.defense.gov/news/d20110714cyber.pdf

Detica report in partnership with the Office of Cyber Security and Information Assurance in the Cabinet Office, "The Cost of Cybercrime", 2011
https://www.gov.uk/government/uploads/system/uploads/attachment_data/file/60943/the-cost-of-cybercrime-full-report.pdf

Edwards, Marty & Stauffer, Todd. "Control Systems Security Assessments: Automation Summit: A Users Conference", 2008
http://graphics8.nytimes.com/packages/pdf/science/NSTB.pdf

Emigh, Aaron. "The Crimeware Landscape: Malware, Phishing, Identity Theft and Beyond", 2006
http://docs.apwg.org/reports/APWG_CrimewareReport.pdf

Council of Europe. "EU Convention on Cybercrime", European Treaty Series No.185, 2001
http://conventions.coe.int/Treaty/en/Treaties/Html/185.htm

Fedorov, Aleksandr V. Russian Academy of Natural Sciences "Information Weapons as a New Means of warfare, " Moscow PIR Conference, 2001

Fisher, Dennis. "NSA Bought Exploit Service From VUPEN, Contract Shows", Threatpost, 2013
http://threatpost.com/nsa-bought-exploit-service-from-vupen-contract-shows

Florêncio, Dinei a.nd Herley, Cormac. "Sex, Lies & Cybercrime Surveys", Microsoft Research, 2011
http://research.microsoft.com/apps/pubs/default.aspx?id=149886

Gorman, Sean P. "Is There A Cybersecurity Threat To National Security? An Interpretive Analysis", 2003
http://gembinski.com/interactive/GMU/research/Cyber_threat_paper.pdf

Greenwald, Glenn. "XKeyscore: NSA Tool Collects 'Nearly Everything A User Does On the Internet", *The Guardian, 2013*
http://www.theguardian.com/world/2013/jul/31/nsa-top-secret-program-online-data

GreyLogic, "Project Grey Goose: Phase II Report – The Evolving State of Cyber Warfare", 2009
http://fserror.com/pdf/GreyGoose2.pdf

Internet Crime Complaint Center (IC3), "Internet Crime Complaint Center Reports", 2001–2012
  http://www.ic3.gov/media/annualreports.aspx

Internet Crime Complaint Center (IC3), "2012 Internet Crime Report", 2012
  http://www.ic3.gov/media/annualreport/2012_IC3Report.pdf

Iomega Corporation, "Disaster Recovery for Small Businesses", Technical White Paper, 2009
  ftp://ftp.iomega.com/resources/whitepapers/ix-dr.pdf

Information Warfare Monitor/Shadowserver Foundation, "Shadows in the Cloud: Investigating Cyber Espionage 2.0", Joint Report JR03–2010, 2010
    http://www.scribd.com/doc/29435784/SHADOWS-IN-THE-CLOUD-Investigating-Cyber espionage-2-0

Kovacs, Eduard. "German Email Security Provider: 750 New PayPal Phishing Sites Spotted Every Day", Softpedia, 2013
    http://news.softpedia.com/news/German-Email-Security-Provider-750-New-PayPal-Phishing-Sites-Spotted-Every-Day-375232.shtml

Lind, Michael. "Stop Pretending Cyberspace Exists", Salon, 2013
  http://www.salon.com/2013/02/12/the_end_of_cyberspace/

Leyden, John. "Cyberwar Report: Israel, Finland Best Prepared for Conflict", The Register, 2012
  http://www.theregister.co.uk/2012/01/31/cyberwar_survey/

Maass, Peter & Rajagopalan, Megha. "Does Cybercrime Really Cost $1 Trillion?" ProPublica, 2012
  http://www.propublica.org/article/does-cybercrime-really-cost-1-trillion

Mele, Stefano. "Cyber weapons: Legal and Strategic Aspects Version 2.0", Italian Institute of Strategic Studies, 2013
    http://www.strategicstudies.it/wp-content/uploads/2013/07/Machiavelli-Editions-Cyber   weapons-Legal-and-Strategic-Aspects-V2.0.pdf

Morris, Nigel. "Operation Tempora: GCHQ in Fresh Snooping Row as it Eavesdrops on Phones and the Internet", The Independent, 2013
    http://www.independent.co.uk/news/uk/politics/operation-tempora-gchq-in-fresh-snooping-row-as-it-eavesdrops-on-phones-and-the-internet-8669137.html

Neal, Ryan W. "FBI Adds Syrian Electronic Army To Wanted List; Supporters Of Hacker Collective Will Be Regarded As Terrorists", International Business Times, 2013
    http://www.ibtimes.com/fbi-adds-syrian-electronic-army-wanted-list-supporters-hacker-collective-will-be-regarded-terrorists

Norton by Symantec, "Norton Cybercrime Report", 2012
    http://nowstatic.norton.com/now/en/pu/images/Promotions/2012/cybercrimeReport/2012_Norton_Cybercrime_Report_Master_FINAL_050912.pdf

Norton-Taylor, Richard & Hopkins, Nick. "Goodbye Squaddies, Hello Hackers", The Guardian, 2013
  http://www.theguardian.com/news/defence-and-security-blog+politics/defence

Osborn, Andrew, & Faulconbridge, Guy. "UK Seeks Full Cyber Warfare Capability", Reuters, 2013
  http://uk.reuters.com/article/2013/09/29/uk-britain-cyber warfare-idUKBRE98S0GK20130929

Pakistani Defense. "New War Between India and Pakistan: Cyber Warfare", Weblog, 2011
http://defence.pk/threads/new-war-between-india-and-pakistan-cyber-warfare.122982/

O'Connor, TJ. "The Jester Dynamic: A Lesson in Asymmetric Unmanaged Cyber Warfare", SANS Institute, 2011
http://www.sans.org/reading-room/whitepapers/attacking/jester-dynamic-lesson-asymmetric-unmanaged-cyber warfare-33889

Ponemon Institute, "2012 Cost of Cybercrime Study: United States", 2012
http://www.ponemon.org/local/upload/file/2012_US_Cost_of_Cyber_Crime_Study_FINAL6%20.pdf

Ponemon Institute, "2013 Cost of Cybercrime Study: United States", 2013
http://media.scmagazine.com/documents/54/2013_us_ccc_report_final_6-1_13455.pdf

Ryan, Thomas. "Getting Into Bed With Robin Sage", 2010
http://media.blackhat.com/bh-us-10/whitepapers/Ryan/BlackHat-USA-2010-Ryan-Getting-In-Bed-With-Robin-Sage-v1.0.pdf

Wolff, Josephine. *Scientific American*, 2011
http://www.scientificamerican.com/article.cfm?id=how-would-us-respond-nightmare-cyber-attack

Schneier, Bruce. "Why Data Mining Won't Stop Terror", Wired, 2006
http://www.wired.com/politics/security/commentary/securitymatters/2006/03/70357?currentPage=all

US Army. "Cyberspace Operations Concept Capability Plan 2016–2028", TRADOC Pamphlet 525–7–8, 2010
http://www.fas.org/irp/doddir/army/pam525-7-8.pdf

US Government. "Information Operations Roadmap", 2003
http://news.bbc.co.uk/1/shared/bsp/hi/pdfs/27_01_06_psyops.pdf

The Week staff, "The $8 Trillion Internet Economy: By the Numbers", 2011
http://theweek.com/article/index/221181/the-8-trillion-internet-economy-by-the-numbers

Waterman, Shaun. "Iran's Cyber Warfare Could Hit Public More than Military: Report", *The Washington Times*, 2013
http://www.washingtontimes.com/news/2013/jul/29/irans-cyber   warfare-could-hit-public-more-military/

Whitehead, Tom. "Americans Pay GCHQ £100m to Spy For Them, Leaked Papers Claim", *Daily Telegraph*, 2013
http://www.telegraph.co.uk/news/uknews/defence/10217280/Americans-pay-GCHQ-100m-to-spy-for-them-leaked-papers-claim.html

INDEX